the
HOUSE
that
CHEESE
BUILT

THE **UNUSUAL LIFE** OF THE **MEXICAN IMMIGRANT** WHO DEFINED A **MULTIBILLION-DOLLAR** GLOBAL INDUSTRY

MIGUEL LEAL

WILEY

Published by John Wiley & Sons, Inc., Hoboken, New Jersey.
Published simultaneously in Canada.

For general information on our other products and services or for technical support, please contact our Customer Care Department within the United States at (800) 762-2974, outside the United States at (317) 572-3993 or fax (317) 572-4002.

Wiley also publishes its books in a variety of electronic formats. Some content that appears in print may not be available in electronic formats. For more information about Wiley products, visit our web site at www.wiley.com.

Library of Congress Control Number is Available:

ISBN 9781394184026 (Cloth)
ISBN 9781394184040 (ePDF)
ISBN 9781394184033 (ePub)

Cover Design: Paul McCarthy
Cover Art: © Shutterstock | Guajillo Studio/Geshas

SKY10051214_072423

I dedicate this book to my mother.

Contents

Acknowledgments

To my children, I am grateful, and I love you.

To my grandparents, my parents, all my brothers and sisters, all their children, and every other member of my extended family, I am thankful.

To those who worked with and for me, in multiple factories across multiple decades, I appreciate all your hard work, dedication, and pride in making the best cheeses in the world.

To all the Amish people of Middlefield, Ohio, thank you for the opportunity.

The following people and organizations were instrumental in my success:

Uncle Joaquin, Eladia Alcaldo, Jorge Reinozo, the Buholzer Family, Darling Dairy Supply, Ted Tooley, Dave Golf, Jim Faith, Mary Olson, Martha Arroyo, Ernesto De la Rosa, Jorge Moreno, and Octavio Constantini.

Enormous thanks to the wonderfully gifted writer Holly Robinson, without whom this book literally would not exist.

And finally, I am so grateful for Tim Dillow, my business partner and friend.

Prologue: The House that Cheese Built

There's hardly a place in this house that I haven't helped craft with my own hands, yet some days it feels like a dream. After all, I could still be in prison, if things had gone differently.

You approach my house along a curving dirt road that leads to a fence draped in purple and white bougainvillea blossoms, passing a fountain as you reach the parking area. Hand-carved wooden doors worthy of a church are set into the house's thick walls, which are built in the traditional hacienda style and keep us cool even in the middle of a Mexican summer.

Inside, the marble floor is cool as well, and the heavy beams and furniture are hand-hewn from exotic woods I've found or bought from different regions of Mexico. There is a modern kitchen because I love to cook and entertain; from the kitchen, you can see the palapa where we often eat outside overlooking the lake and its island. On the island is a statue of Hanuman, the Hindu monkey god known for his ability to conquer impossible odds.

I can relate to that monkey. My journey to this place hasn't been easy.

But my favorite part of this house is the massive hollow tree inside. I've turned that imposing trunk into a tower alongside the staircase that leads to my bedroom. The bathroom adjoins the bedroom, and in there I've placed a copper tub inside another hollow log that I found in the forest—this one the result of a tree being struck by lightning.

Again, I can relate. Being charged with a crime late in my career was like being set on fire.

Outside my room, you can look down through the glass floor and see the face of Zeus carved into the tree, and from the bedroom itself you can open the balcony doors and survey the lake, a vast vegetable garden, and the tidy rows of new avocado trees.

There was no house, lake, or farm before I arrived. I have created them all. This is the house that cheese built.

The lake came first. My brother and I were teaming up on a joint real estate venture, building 150 new homes, and we needed bricks for the construction. I'd already bought this parcel of land; to save a little money, I arranged to dig the earth for manufacturing the bricks from my own property. In seizing the opportunity to save money, I allowed my imagination to conjure the lake from the growing hole in the ground, envisioning how it would be to have my own island in the middle of a lake stocked with fish and frogs, providing a haven for warblers and wrens, hummingbirds and egrets.

Like many things in my life, the tree tower, too, was the product of opportunity and my imagination. Hiking in the jungle of Jalisco one day, I came upon an enormous hollow tree lying in the forest and immediately knew I wanted to create something out of it—even before I had a house. Even if it meant figuring out a way to haul a 25-ton piece of deadwood across the miles.

Entrepreneurs like me are constantly problem solving. We meld opportunity, creativity, and resilience to achieve our goals. Even when things are difficult, our passion pushes us forward until we turn dreams into realities.

I don't have a fancy college degree. In fact, I barely graduated from high school. Nor did I have family money or support. All I have ever had was myself. Yet, I managed to build a multi-million dollar global company, and it all started with cheese.

It nearly all ended with cheese, too, when I was accused by the FDA of manufacturing "dirty" cheese and had to serve time in prison. Who goes to jail for dirty cheese?

Me. That's who.

In my parole letter to the judge who sat my case, I described my family's poverty, and how that drove me to immigrate to the United States as a teenager despite having no skills.

My first night in the United States "I stole two pieces of bread for dinner and then went to sleep in the boiler room of the factory with no bed or blankets or anything else," I wrote. "I spent the first three weeks of the job sleeping there, without the language to ask for help and feeling alone. . . . When I first got paid I walked 13 miles to the nearest store and bought cans of ravioli that I could store and eat in the boiler room."

In pleading my case, I tried to impress upon the judge that cheese is both the passion and profit sum total of my story. Cheese saved my life and helped me build an empire from nothing. It's why I still get up every morning with a burning need to create a new product, like the new recipe for queso fresco I'm currently developing.

There are many rags-to-riches immigrant stories in the United States. What sets mine apart is that my struggles, which I thought were over after I succeeded in bringing my childhood sweetheart from Mexico to the United States and building a successful company by becoming one of the first to make and sell Hispanic-style cheeses, were even more challenging after I sold my business, despite being richer than I'd ever imagined possible.

Just as I began fantasizing about a life of leisure and travel with my family, I received word from the Food and Drug Administration that we had to recall one of our products, and that I might go to prison for selling contaminated cheese. I also discovered my wife was cheating on me.

Prologue: The House that Cheese Built

As I wrote in that parole letter to the judge, "I sank into a world completely unfamiliar to myself."

In a matter of weeks, I lost my wife, my passport, and my freedom. Suicide seemed like the only way out, and so I cut my wrists, prepared to end it all. That's when I learned that sometimes you can only discover where you truly belong if you touch bottom first.

As I concluded in my letter, "I show myself in front of you with the most honesty as possible. . .I ask for your mercy and for you to understand what I have done, and to give me a sentence that is reflecting the wrong that I did. I sincerely hope that you will consider my entire life—my whole story—when you give me my sentence."

In reading this book, you will be my judge as well. I will reveal myself to you, too, by sharing my personal and professional journey. More importantly, I'll show you my recipe for paying attention to opportunity and teach you how it's possible to learn as much from your failures as from your successes.

The bottom line is that success and happiness are within your grasp, no matter where you are on your life's journey—at the top, in the middle, or clinging to what feels like the last rung of a shaky ladder. Achieving financial stability and personal contentment means being willing to try something new and recognizing the importance of your own self-worth. You must also allow yourself to break through the barriers you've created to keep yourself "safe" so you can start a new chapter in your life—one that is truly built around *your* choices. By doing this, you will reach a state of grace, accepting whatever comes your way and turning new obstacles into opportunities.

In English, there are so many slang terms for money, many of them food-related: bread, dough, clams, bacon, and "cheese," which was first used as a term for money back in the mid-1800s and was still being used in the 1990s, especially in prominent hip-hop lyrics, like the chorus of Jay-Z's 1999 song, 'Big Pimpin','" where he revels in "spendin' cheese."

For over 40 years, I have followed wherever cheese led me. Cheese has meant not only money but hope for the future. Now my goal is to feed the business instincts and creative minds of future breadwinners like you by telling you all about the house that cheese built.

Part I

CASTAWAY

Chapter 1

Death of the Transformer

Passion Can Find You When You Least Expect It.

Standing in that foggy doorway of the makeshift morgue in Mexico City, I reminded myself that the smoke I saw rising from the bodies had nothing to do with spirits; it was the result of the corpses being stored on dry ice in this humid room. Dry ice is made of frozen carbon dioxide gas, and when it warms, the carbon dioxide creates fog as its temperature rises.

My brother Carlos and I hesitated at the entrance, overcome by horror and fear. What if our father really was lying there among the bodies? Finally we agreed to flip a coin to see who would enter that dark hell.

Carlos lost the bet. But as he was about to step into the warehouse, I moved forward, motivated by a powerful desire to give my mother some peace by bringing our father home to bury him. At the last minute, I asked the guy at the entrance for some cotton dipped in alcohol and put that up my nose, then went in search of my dad by flashlight.

As I wandered through the fog among the dead bodies stacked haphazardly around me, I was tempted to hold my breath to avoid inhaling the scent of death, just as I'd done as a child of eight, when Carlos had convinced me to sneak into a morgue near our house.

"Otherwise, you're a pussy and can't hang around with us anymore, Miguel," he'd said.

Carlos was the ringleader for my gang of brothers. He wasn't the oldest of my five siblings, but he was the bravest. He'd been beaten the most by our father, who beat all of us as well as our mother. My sister was so terrified of our father that she frequently wet her pants when he came home in a drunken rage, his personality so altered by alcohol that we called him "The Transformer."

I'd always wanted to be just like Carlos: courageous and strong. Consequently, I usually did whatever Carlos said, desperate to win his approval. As the youngest of the brothers, I held the lowest rank on our family totem pole. The others made it clear that I didn't have the right to speak and had to always listen to their opinions. I always had to follow their plans, too; if I messed up, I would get teased mercilessly or even beaten up by my older brothers. I quickly learned it was better to observe and keep quiet than to speak up or argue. Those childhood lessons taught me to listen, observe, and never give up.

So, when Carlos told me I had to go into the morgue and see a dead body, I heard my eight-year-old-self agreeing to the plan. We had followed the ambulance one day as it pulled up in front of the morgue, where the men opened the back of the van and pulled out the body on a stretcher to wheel it inside. Then we ran around the side of the building to a big window.

Carlos had given me a shove. "Go!" he hissed. "Don't come back unless you touch a dead body. Remember to hold your breath, Miguel, or you'll breathe in the smell of dead bodies, and it'll kill you!"

I had scrambled through the window and dropped like a cat onto the linoleum floor, where the stink made my eyes water. Men were already working on the body, which was laid out on a metal table. The men were using the body as an ashtray for the cigarettes they were smoking as they opened up the corpse. The guts seemed to literally leap out of the body, and I had gasped, breathing in the foul stink.

I raced out of there, crying, terrified I was going to die because I'd inhaled the smell of death, and went straight home to my mother.

"I'm going to die! I smelled death, and now I'm dying!" I had wailed.

Carlos couldn't stop laughing at me, but I was so hysterical that my mother had called the doctor to come over. He'd reassured me that it was a chemical called formaldehyde I'd inhaled, not death itself. "It can't kill you, Miguel," he'd said, and even uncapped a small bottle of formaldehyde so I could smell it.

Now, as I searched for my father's body among the corpses piled around me following the Mexico City earthquake, I found myself wishing I were as deeply Roman Catholic as the rest of my family. I might have felt some comfort then, thinking these souls were now in heaven, but I couldn't pretend to be religious. Religious people are too often like wolves in sheep's clothing: hypocrites who make you believe they're good people, when underneath they're no better than the rest of us.

Most of the bodies had been terribly disfigured by being trapped beneath the rubble after the earthquake. Carlos and I had arrived in Mexico City after hearing the news, knowing our father was staying in a hotel there; a bus had dropped us off on the outskirts and we'd walked another hour through the pitch-black city to a friend's house. It was like walking through an apocalypse, with the constant sound of sirens screaming, the acrid scent of smoke, and people digging through the fallen buildings for bodies. I kept imagining the ground opening up beneath our feet and swallowing us whole.

Now I saw not only bodies, but severed fingers sticking up from buckets; some of the fingers still had wedding rings. Other body parts—a piece of an ear, a foot, a nose—were scattered on the floor, waiting to be recognized. Some of the corpses had also begun to decompose. Fortunately, the alcohol-drenched cotton did the trick, and I was able to get through the experience without passing out.

5

Death of the Transformer

For the next week, Carlos and I, along with others in our family, frantically searched Mexico City's temporary morgues, hoping my father might miraculously surprise us by showing up alive. How was it possible that a man who'd seemed so terrifyingly invincible to us could be dead?

But it was clear from seeing how little was left of the hotel that most of the staff and clients hadn't made it out alive. At one point, a morgue attendant showed us a body so battered by building debris that we couldn't tell if the person was male or female. When the attendant tried to open the mouth of the corpse to check the teeth, the cheek opened up and the overpowering stink of rot caused my insides to heave.

At last we gave up our search. I returned to Guanajuato, grief-stricken and exhausted, and resumed mastering the art of making cheese. It felt like the only thing in my life I could control.

■ ■ ■

I was making cheese on the day my father died. It wasn't quite 7.30 a.m. on that September morning in 1985 when I had shut off the agitator after curdling a tub of Oaxaca cheese, a white, semi-soft cheese made from cow's milk that's similar to mozzarella.

To my surprise, the agitator continued shaking for several minutes after I turned it off.

The guys working with me had joked about the trembling. "Must be an earthquake," one said.

We all laughed. We have a lot of earthquakes in Mexico. Most are nothing to worry about, so I continued performing my tasks.

I'd recently graduated from high school and was apprenticing at Productos Lacteos Blanquita, a cheese factory in Irapuato, my hometown in the Mexican state of Guanajuato. School was never my thing. I suffered from dyslexia and attention issues, though I didn't know it then, since nobody ever diagnosed it. Whenever my teachers asked

The House that Cheese Built

me to read aloud, I'd pretend to know the words, leading the other children to laugh and mock me.

By junior high, I'd discovered that my survival depended on being the class clown and tougher than anyone else. This was easy, since I had a father and four older brothers dedicated to fighting each other. I'd learned how to throw punches early, and I'd been suspended or expelled from school various times for fooling around or engaging in more serious misbehavior, like setting a desk on fire.

I'd been held back twice in seventh grade and, in high school, spent more time with my girlfriend, carousing with friends, and drinking than on academics. I managed to graduate only by bribing various teachers and had taken the job at the cheese factory simply for the paycheck.

That night, I had arrived home after work and turned on the news. That's when I learned there really *had* been an earthquake. It was no ordinary Mexican tremor, either; with a magnitude of 8.1, the quake that morning was the most violent to hit the Western Hemisphere this century. Since most of the damage was in Mexico City, however, it seemed like a tragic but distant event that had nothing to do with my daily life.

It wasn't until Carlos had come to find me that I realized the disaster had struck close to home, killing my father. We never did find his body, but the event changed my life nonetheless.

■ ■ ■

My girlfriend, Martina, did her best to comfort me after my father's death, but it was difficult because she'd already left for the university in Guadalajara. I'd met her, when I was 17 and she was 15, one night when I was competing in a shooting competition. I'd been learning to shoot since early childhood, when my beloved abuelo, Jose Pepe, my mother's father and an engineer educated in the United States, enthusiastically taught me how to make a slingshot by finding

Death of the Transformer

a Y-shaped piece of wood, then cutting off the back of a shoe to use as the pouch, which we attached to the Y with rubber tubing. (He was less enthusiastic when he later discovered me diligently cutting up all of the shoes in his closet to make multiple slingshots.)

I admired Don Jose Pepe more than anyone. He had been raised in the United States and returned to Mexico to marry my grandmother, where they had a big hacienda. He'd made a good living as the owner of a laminated cardboard factory before he retired.

Don Jose Pepe's stories became myths in my imagination. My favorite was about the time my grandfather had been shot in the elbow by a bandit while riding horseback on his property. He'd fallen off his horse and into the mud near a river. When he heard the hoof beats of the bandit's horses racing toward him, my grandfather stuck his elbow in the mud to staunch the bleeding and hid underwater, using a reed as a straw so he could breathe. Later, his arm was operated on and the shattered elbow was removed, which meant he could bend his arm in any direction.

"Abuelo! You can do magic!" I'd exclaim every time I saw his arm flop over in strange ways.

Don Jose Pepe gave me my first BB gun. I quickly learned to love the precision of shooting at targets early on and the absolute mental focus it takes to hit the center. I had no money to buy my own rifle or even ammunition, but when I was a teenager, my friend Octavio's father sometimes sponsored me for competitions.

The night I met Martina, I was competing at our local gun club in Irapuato and took second place. As Octavio and I were celebrating my victory, he pointed out his cousin Martina, who smiled at us from across the field.

What did I see, that first night, that would set me squarely on the path to my future? What makes someone fall in love with one person, and not another?

I still have no answers to those questions. I only know that Martina was a petite blonde with pretty features and a smile that seemed to light up the night sky. I went over to talk to her, and before the night was over, she'd kissed me and changed my whole life. I'd kissed girls before, but nothing was as electrifying as Martina's lips on mine.

"That's the girl I'm going to marry," I told Octavio that night. That decision changed the course of my life forever, as she became my mirror, the way I would see myself for many years to come.

Martina and I began dating, though it was more like a game of hide-and-seek: we'd meet in secret anywhere we could to talk and laugh and have sex, even in my brother Carlos's warehouse, where he stored the blue jeans he made in his factory. Blue jeans, it turns out, make a perfectly comfortable mattress.

The reason we had to keep our relationship a secret wasn't just because we were having sex—though that was reason enough, since premarital sex was considered sinful by Mexican Catholic families like ours—but because Martina's parents didn't want her to have anything to do with me. Irapuato was a small town, one where everybody knows everything. Yes, I was a handsome kid, six feet tall and light-skinned with blue eyes, and my family was well educated. Everyone knew Don Jose Pepe had prospered as an engineer and factory owner, and that my other grandfather, my father's father, was a taciturn military doctor. My mother, too, was well-respected as a beautiful woman and devout Catholic. She'd married my father straight out of high school.

And that was the problem: everyone in town knew that my father, despite having so many advantages in life, was an abusive alcoholic who'd begun cheating on my mother the first year of their marriage. He never had a desire to build a career or care for a family. Because of his alcoholism, we were so poor that we would have been homeless if my grandfather hadn't sheltered us in his house and in other apartments he owned around town.

I couldn't rely on my father to be sober and rational, never mind provide me with anything. I never had a pair of shoes or clothing that wasn't handed down from my older brothers, sometimes many times over. If my mother didn't take me and my little sister into the kitchen, away from my brothers, there wouldn't be enough food for me, either.

Martina's family wasn't rich, but they owned a dairy farm, had a car, and were good, steady workers. My family had next to nothing, and I'd earned a reputation as a restless kid who had been held back in school and loved to party.

When I first showed up at their house to take Martina on a date, her mother looked me up and down, taking in my worn jeans and scuffed shoes, and said, "We've got plenty of work you can do around here, Miguel. You could start by mucking out the cow barns and helping us milk. We pay a decent wage."

I seethed at her obvious attempt to put me down and communicate exactly what she thought of me: that I was too low-life for their daughter. People often judge others by how much money you have or what social circles you run in, and Martina's mother was determined to keep me in my place. What she couldn't see was that, because of the hardships I'd suffered as a little kid, I'd become stubborn and determined—traits that would serve me well in years to come. But I put on a charming smile and nodded.

"I'd be pleased to help out with anything you need," I said, "but of course I couldn't accept any money. I'll gladly help you for free."

Boy, did it make me happy to see her face turn bright red with anger at my response.

Martina didn't care that I was poor. Even when she decided to study computer science at the University of Guadalajara, where her parents probably hoped she'd find a better husband, she and I made plans to be together forever. The more her parents tried to push us apart, the more we wanted to be together.

The House that Cheese Built

Martina made me feel accepted in a way I'd never felt at school or even in my own family. She saw my creativity and boundless energy—qualities that had made me a restless troublemaker in the classroom—as positive attributes and believed me when I promised to do great things in the world and take care of her. For my part, I fell in love with Martina's quick mind. She never had trouble with reading and writing like I did, and she was incredibly organized. Like many people who fall in love, we were attracted to one another as opposites, because we filled in each other's gaps.

I suppose, too, that even though I was never much of a practicing Catholic, I'd absorbed some of my mother's beliefs. She'd taught me it was a sacred thing for a woman to give her body to a man. Because I'd taken Martina's virginity, I believed we were bonded, body and soul, for the rest of our lives.

Early in our relationship, Martina called me at one point in tears, saying she'd missed her period and thought she might be pregnant. I freaked out enough to tell my mother.

"Oh, Miguel, what the heck have you done?" my mother moaned. "You know you have to be responsible for that baby now."

"I know, but I'm really scared." I was only 18 and had no idea how I'd support a family.

"Well, you should have thought of that before," my mother said grimly. "You're going to have to marry that girl now."

A few days went by. Finally I went to see Martina. "Listen, do you want to get married?" I asked. "I love you and want to do the right thing."

Martina smiled. "It's okay, Miguel. My period wasn't late. I was just testing you to see your reaction. I wanted to know if you really loved me."

"You're not pregnant?" I asked in shock.

"No," she said. "Everything's okay."

Death of the Transformer

I held her close and kissed her hard, so relieved that I felt like I was floating. I loved Martina, but I wasn't ready to be a father. When I went home and told my mother, though, her reaction floored me.

"You can't see that girl again, Miguel," she said. "She tricked you! You need to get your life together and figure out what you really want."

Her advice was sound. However, my mother's way of teaching me a lesson was to send me on a five-day retreat with the monks in a nearby seminary. I was supposed to focus on Jesus and recognize my mistakes, but after two days of having to pray first thing in the morning, before every meal, and again before I went to bed at night, I was ready to run back to Martina and fled the seminary.

Happiness is defined differently by each of us. For me, it has always come from having dreams and following them. Rather than accept whatever life doles out, or lean on God to provide for me, I prefer to hold the reins and steer my life toward accomplishing the goals that will make my dreams come true. My dream as a teenager was nothing more specific than finding a way to put the past firmly behind me.

For Martina, for my love and respect for her, I vowed to be a better man than my father had ever been. Marrying Martina was a step toward achieving my first dream. Everything I did, I did for my love of her. In my innocence, I believed this would be my surest path to happiness.

But what could I do to make my dream of marrying Martina come true with only a sketchy high school education and no money for college or even trade school?

When my brother Pedro mentioned that his future father-in-law, Don Poncho, needed help at his cheese factory, I jumped at the chance. I'd become friends with Don Poncho's son, Poncho, who was Pedro's age and halfway through his engineering studies, because Poncho was dating Martina's sister, Susanna. (Irapuato really was a small town.) If I worked at the cheese factory, Poncho would be my boss. Better yet, he had a car and could drive me to Guadalajara on weekends, where Martina was living with Susanna while they went to the university.

And so I went to the factory, Productos Lacteos Blanquita, one day and found Don Poncho in his office. "Can you teach me to make cheese?" I asked.

To be clear, I had no ambition to become a cheesemaker. Not yet. At that point, I had no work ethic or clear career goals. I only knew that I didn't want to be a lost dreamer like my father, who often outlined grand plans for getting rich on napkins when he was sober enough to hold a pencil, but never followed through because the bottle got the best of him.

The work weeks dragged by. La Blanquita's headquarters was a warehouse with a door that opened onto the receiving area where all of the trucks were loaded. On the right side of the warehouse, where I worked, was the production side, with a pasteurizer, a 5,000-lb. cheese vat, the homogenizer, and a special grinder to make the cheeses. On the right side of the warehouse were the stored barrels and bags of vegetable oil, flour, whey, and stabilizers, as well as the boiler room and compressor for the coolers. The whole place stank like a sewer; I accepted the stink at the time as the way all cheese factories must smell.

Don Poncho specialized in Oaxaca cheese. It's a stringy cheese, as I discovered in the factory—you can literally stretch it out when it's hot, like gum, then cut it and roll it into a ball—and one of the most popular cheeses in Mexico. The other cheese he sold was a queso fresco that we made from a paste.

My job was to follow the recipes and check to make sure the products were consistent. Don Poncho owned the factory, but he knew little about the actual cheese production; he left that to his employees, who taught me. The milk arrived in 40-gallon cans, and

13

Death of the Transformer

my first job was to set the milk with rennet, an enzyme added to make the milk coagulate before putting in liquid calcium. Don Poncho added a lot of other products to the milk to increase his yield, like potato flour and other stabilizers, and put everything through a homogenizer to make the cheese set. I simply accepted this process as the way cheese was made. What did I know? Less than nothing.

I was on my feet all day in the heat while Poncho and Don Poncho worked in the air-conditioned offices out back. One of the worst jobs was stretching the Oaxaca cheese by hand, then rolling the gummy strings of cheese into balls for the marketplace. The cheese was steaming hot, and I routinely suffered burns and blisters on my palms.

My salary was low, just 120 pesos per week (about $7.50 US), but at least the employees took a lot of breaks. I lounged with the rest of them, eating tortas of cheese and avocados and telling jokes. Nobody seemed to supervise the work, and nobody ever seemed to get fired. Some mornings we might work for only an hour before taking a break. I convinced myself that this job was fine for now, and someday I'd do better—though I had no plan.

Anyway, I was living for the weekends. Every Friday, Poncho was waiting for me with the car, ready to whisk me away to Guadalajara, where he paid for the hotel so we could sleep with Susanna and Martina. He paid, too, for nearly everything else we did—movies, clubs, dinners—though he always made sure to let me know how much I owed him.

Once, for instance, our friend Chavin stopped by the factory, and when I offered him a 1-kg piece of cheese to take home and taste because I was excited to see what he thought of it, Poncho stopped me.

"Miguel, you fuck, you have to pay me for that cheese. You can't just give it away!"

I disguised my fury and reached into my pocket for the money. "Here," I said, and handed it to Poncho. "Take the cheese, Chavin. I really want to know what you think."

Always, I thanked Poncho whenever he paid for me, and was grateful, while at the same time vowing that someday I would be the one who paid for my friends.

■ ■ ■

Seeing how distraught I was after my father's death, Don Poncho, the owner of La Blanquita, asked if I wanted to travel south to Tierra Caliente in the state of Michoacán to apprentice with his friend Don Vicente. As sad as I was to move even farther away from Martina in Guadalajara, I welcomed the idea. Don Vicente was a third-generation cheesemaker who specialized in producing Cotija cheese, something I had yet to learn.

The history of cheese in Mexico began with the Spanish conquest, when the Spanish brought dairy animals—cattle, sheep, and goats—as well as cheese-making techniques to my country. During colonial times, cheese making changed to suit the different European and indigenous tastes. Distinct varieties of cheese were made in each region of Mexico, almost all of them from cow's milk.

Today, Mexico is rated 10th in the world for cheese production, with probably 50 unique varieties of cheese. Some, like Oaxaca cheese, are made in every part of Mexico, while others are regional cheeses known only in specific parts of the country. Certain cheeses, like panela and Chihuahua, are made with pasteurized milk and are mass-produced, but most are made locally with raw milk.

Cotija, the cheese I was going to make with Don Vicente, is made from raw cow's milk and is named after the town of the same name in the state of Michoacán. It's a white cheese, with a firm texture and a sour smell. The taste is both salty and milky. Typically the cheese is aged about a year, which takes care of any bacteria, and sometimes the wheels are covered in chili pepper paste. Young cotija cheese is moist and crumbly, similar to Greek feta. If it's aged longer, cotija turns sharper in taste and becomes harder, so that it's more similar

15

Death of the Transformer

to Parmesan. It's beloved by Mexicans as a finishing touch on pretty much anything from enchiladas to posole.

Don Poncho gave me Don Vicente's address in Uruapan, Michoacán, and sent me there by bus. Uruapan is a lush, green city known for its river and stunning Tzararacua waterfall. Unfortunately, I wasn't touring the waterfall but stuck on a local bus that stopped at every hint of a village, seated next to a native woman in a wide skirt who chose to relieve herself in the bus aisle.

My stomach was churning from the smell and the jolting bus ride by the time I arrived at the stop closest to the cheese factory, where I finally met Don Vicente. His car was small, but the man himself was massive, probably close to 400 pounds. It was a miracle he didn't get stuck behind the steering wheel.

But Don Vicente was very kind. He invited me to dinner at his house and gave me a room to stay in. The room was in a building still under construction; he locked me inside.

"For your own safety," he said, and promised to pick me up early the next morning to take me to the factory.

The apartment was well appointed and comfortable. Unfortunately, in the middle of the night I was awakened when the earth started rumbling beneath me. An earthquake!

Through the window, I was shocked to see that the sky was filling with smoke and ash. It dawned on me then that it wasn't an earthquake, but a volcanic eruption. Later I'd learn it was from Nevado de Colima, in nearby Nevado National Park, which contains some of Mexico's most active volcanoes. I began shouting frantically, haunted by memories of the disfigured corpses I'd seen in Mexico City and convinced I was about to be buried in lava.

"Let me out!" I shouted, over and over. "Help, I'm trapped. Let me out!"

There was no one to hear my screams. At last I spotted a space in the roof big enough for me to squeeze between the roof and the

The House that Cheese Built

top of the gate. I managed to heave my skinny body through the gap and fell two stories down to the ground, where I lay there, shaking. A neighbor woman tried to rouse me, but I stayed there until Don Vicente showed up some hours later.

I returned home immediately, too traumatized to even speak to my family about what had happened, but returned to Don Vicente's a week later, determined to learn whatever he could teach me.

■ ■ ■

The next time I arrived in Uruapan, I managed to take a direct bus to the station closest to Don Vicente's house. I carried everything I needed in my backpack: clothes, a notebook to write down whatever I observed and learned, and a pH meter to track the acidity of the cheese. What I really wanted to study was the chemistry. I wanted to know what was actually happening with the cotija cheese to gradually produce its trademark acidity and flavor.

That first morning, Don Vicente drove me to the factory. After saying goodbye to his wife—a surprisingly petite, trim woman for such an enormous husband—his first question was, "Do you want to have breakfast? Maybe an orange juice?"

"Sure," I said, so he stopped at a juice stand.

"How big, and how many raw eggs in it?" Don Vicente asked.

"Just a medium juice without an egg," I said.

He laughed and, after handing me my juice, ordered his own: five liters of juice with raw eggs. Don Vicente tore a corner in the juice bag with his teeth and said, "Look, Miguelito, I'm going to chug five liters of orange juice with raw eggs for strength," he said and did just that.

Minutes later, we stopped near some train tracks. "There are some very good tacos there," Don Vicente said, pointing to a taco truck near the tracks. "You want some tacos, Miguelito?"

"Well, sure, Don Vicente."

Death of the Transformer

"Good. Come on, then. How many?"

"Give me five," I said.

"And something to drink?"

"A Coke would be great, thanks."

The taco seller seemed to know Don Vicente well, smiling and greeting him by name. When I heard Don Vicente order his own tacos—20 of them, with double tortillas, along with a family-size Coke—I nearly died laughing, but managed to stop myself in time. I watched in amazement as he ate them all in minutes.

"Miguelito," he said, "Do you want some more tacos?"

"No, Don Vicente."

"Well, I fucking do," he said, and ordered 15 more with another family-size Coke.

Two giant sodas and 35 tacos later, Don Vicente stuck a toothpick in his mouth and we drove on. As we neared Tierra Caliente some 45 minutes later, he shouted, "Miguelito, how about a beer and some French fries?"

Jesus, I thought, noting my new boss's sweaty red face and labored breathing. *This guy might die of a heart attack before we even get to the factory.* But what could I do but agree? So we stopped at a store, where I asked for a six-pack of beer. Then we picked up a couple of bags of French fries.

After that, we crossed a river and arrived at Don Vicente's hacienda, where I hoped he'd finally reveal the secrets of making perfect cotija cheese.

How odd, when I reflect back on that early chapter in my life now, to think that all I wanted at the time was a job that would help me survive the disaster of my father's death and the mess I'd made of my own education and life so far. But this was one of the most important lessons of my life: sometimes we don't find our passions. Our passions find us—often when we least expect it. All we have to do is be open and pay attention to new opportunities.

Chapter 2

Desire More

To Succeed in Business, You Have to Want to Improve Your Life.

Don Vicente's cheese-making operation was completely different from Don Poncho's. It was a small farm, and where Don
Poncho relied mostly on vegetable oil for his recipes, Don Vicente's
cotija cheese was made with 100% milk.

"No vegetable oil at all?" I asked in shock.

"None," he said. "If you put vegetable oil in this cheese, it will
never age."

The cows were milked in the morning, and the milk was delivered that afternoon, which meant the cheese had to be processed
right away or the milk would spoil.

To my relief, Don Vicente's cheese factory didn't smell as bad
as Don Poncho's, and everything was better organized. And, unlike
Don Poncho, Don Vicente actually worked in his own factory. He
knew a lot about making cotija cheese and carefully explained every
step to me. His hands-on lessons would eventually lead me to success beyond my wildest imaginings, though of course I didn't know
that yet. He taught me about pasteurization and homogenization and
about the acidity of different cheeses.

I'd never been much of a student because of my learning dis-
abilities, but I'd always been naturally curious, a great observer, and
a hands-on learner. To learn to observe, you first need to master
patience. Many times, people answer when someone is talking, trying

to finish the ideas of the other person. It's better to listen and observe and earn the right to speak.

The chemistry of cheese making fascinated me. I probably learned more in one day from Don Vicente than I had in the nine months I'd already spent with Don Poncho and Poncho at La Blanquita.

To make the cotija, Don Vicente showed me how to add salt and a little bit of calcium to the raw milk, then rennet to help coagulate the milk into cheese.

"Never use vegetable oil in cotija," he repeated.

After the cheese was dry, we lay it out on long wooden processing tables to cut slices into the cheese. This allowed the acidity to rise in the heat, killing the bacteria and developing the flavor as the cotija continued to age and dry out. The cheese was aged at least 60 days before selling it, which not only added to the flavor, but made it safe to eat, particularly because it's so hot in this part of Mexico that we call it "Tierra Caliente."

■ ■ ■

A few months after I left Don Vicente and returned to work at La Blanquita, it became clear that I was stuck. I wasn't learning any new skills, and I was spending my nights and weekends partying hard. When you are raising yourself, with no parents to guide you, your friends become your family. And if you have friends who are drinking and drifting without purpose, as I did then, it's easy to get caught up in the chaos and lose yourself in the crowd and forget to set goals. When your parents don't teach you, your friends polish your personality. You can't escape this pattern unless you recognize it, and that is nearly impossible because it means leaving the only family you have.

Poncho and I had already managed to crash his dad's truck after one endless night of drinking. I couldn't pursue any other sort of professional career without an education, but there was no money for school, and I had no head for academics anyway. At this rate,

I'd never earn much more than 120 pesos a week. I had no hope of saving money for an engagement ring, never mind marrying Martina. I was in despair. How could I ever prove myself worthy as a husband to Martina and her family?

The answer, when it came, would change the course of my life again. Don Poncho, in one of his alcohol-fueled rants with Poncho and me, said, "I need to make American cheese! Everyone in Mexico imports American cheddar, but we could make it cheaper. We just need to know how."

"So send us to America, *Papi*," Poncho joked.

I joined in. "Sure, we can teach the Americans about Mexican cheese in exchange."

The three of us looked at each other and burst into laughter, raising our bottles of beer to toast our own brilliance. The laughter made me bold.

"Don Poncho, my mother has a friend living in Chicago," I said. "Let's ask him to help us."

My mother's friend, Jorge Reinosa, was buying cheddar for his store and restaurant from the Klondike cheese factory in Wisconsin. To my shock, within weeks of contacting Jorge, we had an agreement between Klondike and La Blanquita to exchange cheese recipes and techniques. Poncho and I would travel there as part of this exchange of knowledge.

"We'll teach them to make cheese the Mexican way, and you'll learn the American way," Don Poncho said, slapping us on the shoulders. "Pack your bags, boys. You're going north."

No matter how scared I was about traveling to the United States, I knew it was my only way forward. There was nothing for me in Mexico. No money, no education, no opportunities to make something of myself. Martina and my other friends were leaving me far behind. This was it, my big break. But my excitement was dampened by my feelings of apprehension and grief about leaving Martina behind. I couldn't bear spending even a weekend without her. How would I last for months? And what if she fell in love with someone else while I was gone?

"I'll be earning plenty of US dollars," I assured Martina on my next visit to Guadalajara, though I had no idea what my salary would be. "As soon as I have enough saved, I'll bring you to the United States. We can get married and spend a year there before coming back."

"Really?" Martina's eyes were bright with excitement as she kissed me. "What an adventure! I'm so proud of you, Miguel!"

Her belief in me was like flames under my feet. I was determined to succeed in the United States, and to find my next big opportunity. I had to do it for Martina. For us. She was my whole life.

"I love you," I said, and scooped her into my arms to carry her into the bedroom.

She pressed her face against my neck. "I love you more," she said.

■ ■ ■

When my Uncle Joaquin heard about my upcoming trip, he convinced me that I needed to study English before leaving. "Otherwise, you will be completely lost," he said. "How can you learn anything in the United States if you don't speak the language?"

Uncle Joaquin was my father's brother, but he was everything my father was not: a tall, good looking, successful businessman with a firm handshake and a thick head of dark hair. He was the one I'd always gone to whenever I needed help or advice, since I couldn't rely on my father for anything. My last conversation with my father had taken place a few weeks before he died in the earthquake, when I'd tried talking to him about what I might be able to do to get Martina's mother to like me, or at least accept me.

"I want to marry Martina, but I don't think her mother will ever agree," I had confided. "She doesn't think I'm good enough for Martina."

The House that Cheese Built

My father had laughed and said, "You know what you need to do, Miguelito?"

"No, what?" I had asked hopefully. If nothing else, my father was an expert with women.

"You need to sleep with her!" he'd said, roaring with laughter. "Sleep with your future mother-in-law, and all of your problems with her will melt away!"

At that moment, I knew for a fact that I could never lean on my father again.

Uncle Joaquin, on the other hand, was not only reliable and wise about things like politics and business, but my life saver—literally. It had happened when I was about seven years old. Uncle Joaquin owned a boat, and one hot Sunday he had invited my family to join his on the shores of a small lake in San Miguel de Allende.

"Come on, we'll picnic and swim and have fun," he'd said. "Maybe I'll even get you up on water skis."

That afternoon had started out promising enough, with all of us splashing around in the water and taking turns trying to ski, hooting with laughter when we fell. It was one of the best days of my life until it turned into one of the worst.

At some point in the afternoon, my father had crossed the line, as he always did, from drinking to drunk, and became The Transformer. I could always tell when this happened because his face turned red and his voice got louder and angrier. We'd been watching another boat with a pair of guys in it; they kept going out to the middle of the lake with their dog, a black lab, and tossing the dog off the boat so it could swim back to shore. I suppose that's what gave my father the idea to command Carlos and me into the boat.

"Come on, you curs!" he shouted. "Let's go have some fun!"

We knew better than to argue. Carlos and I followed him down to the dock, hoping one of the adults might notice and stop him, or at least come with us. Nobody did. They were all gathered around the coolers of food and picnic tables, oblivious to our departure.

My father took the boat out at top speed. Carlos and I shivered in the wind and clung to the rail. Then, without warning, my father abruptly cut the engine and yelled, "C'mon! Jump! I want to see you swim to shore!"

Carlos and I looked at each other in panic. We were in the middle of the lake. "Papa, no," Carlos said.

My father's face had turned even redder, something I didn't think was possible. "What did you say?"

Carlos stood up. He was nearly as tall as our father, but skinny like a heron. I desperately wanted him to hit my father at that moment, to knock him right out of the boat. As we rode across the lake, I had been remembering night in Mexico City when I was probably six years old. We were living in a tall white apartment building in one of the nicer sections of the city, but the apartment was tiny. There was barely enough room in the kitchen for us to sit around the table. My parents slept in one bedroom with my little sister, while we boys were crowded into bunk beds in the other room.

That night, I had cowered with my siblings in the living room while our parents fought in the kitchen. I was too young to understand what they were shouting at each other—it was probably about another woman, knowing my father's habits—but my father was drunk and throwing kitchen chairs at my mother while she cried and screamed. Carlos had run into the kitchen and stood between my parents, taking the beating to save our mother.

But Carlos didn't look like my brave older brother at that moment in the boat. He was pale and trembling hard, his teeth chattering as he stepped up onto the bench, held his nose, and jumped into the water.

"You're next, Miguel!" my father had bellowed. "You saw that dog swim to shore. You can do it, too. Come on. Swim like a dog!"

I was terrified. I knew how to swim, but the afternoon had turned cloudy and chilly. The lake shore looked a million miles away, my family like ants around the picnic tables.

As scary and cold as that lake looked, however, the anger in my father's eyes was even more terrifying. He would beat me bloody if I didn't jump. There was nobody here to protect me, so I followed Carlos into the water. We both started paddling toward shore, our teeth chattering, our father laughing like a maniac as he started the boat up again and roared past us.

The thing about lakes is that sound easily carries across them. It wasn't long before my father reached the shore and I heard my Uncle Joaquin shouting at him. "What the fuck do you think you're doing, leaving the boys so far out in the water like that?" he yelled.

Minutes later—an infinity of minutes, as I imagined lake monsters grabbing at my legs and pulling me under—the boat returned. This time Uncle Joaquin was at the wheel. He leaned over to haul us into the boat, wrapped us in dry towels, then sped back to shore, where our mother was in tears and our father was nowhere in sight. That was the last time our family ever received an invitation to go boating on the lake.

Now, when Uncle Joaquin heard about me going to the United States, he came to my rescue once again by offering to sign me up for an English course. "The thing is, you'll have to go to Mexico City to take this intensive language course," he said.

"But I don't have any money," I said.

"Don't worry," he said. "I'll pay for it."

A week later, I was on a bus to the capitol with 3,000 pesos in my pocket. I'd never felt so rich. I chose a seat on the bus next to a priest. At least, I assumed he was a priest because he was wearing a clerical collar, which was partly why I'd chosen that particular seat.

When the bus stopped in San Juan del Rio to let the passengers off for breakfast, though, that "priest" saw the wallet in my pocket and tried to grab it. I punched him in the face and ran; I knew there would be no other money if I lost Joaquin's investment in me.

In Mexico City, I rented a room in the apartment of a woman who worked all day. My teachers assured me the United States was every bit as beautiful and rich as the America I saw on television and in the movies. "People in the United States are so wealthy compared to Mexico, you can live off the garbage, Miguel," they told me. "There are opportunities to make money everywhere."

This excited my imagination. If I could make money, surely I could bring Martina to live with me in the United States soon. We'd marry and start a family and save enough money to buy a nice house in Mexico.

Clinging to that fantasy got me through the next six months of English classes. I was in school only three hours a day, and I didn't do any better at studying or memorizing than I ever had. It was a disaster, really, though I wouldn't realize how little English I'd learned until I arrived north of the border. Meanwhile, I had so much free time that I physically ached for Martina during every minute I wasn't in class. The weekdays dragged by. Most Fridays, I made the long trip by bus to see Martina in Guadalajara.

Once, I was so desperate to see her that I actually spent some of my uncle's precious pesos to fly to Guadalajara from Mexico City. Poncho picked me up at the airport and drove me to Martina's apartment. Susanna was home, but Martina was out.

"Out where?" I asked, bewildered. Somehow, in my fevered imagination, Martina was always waiting to see me, just as I longed to see her, and had nothing better to do than miss me.

Susanna looked uncomfortable. "She went to Lake Chapala with a bunch of friends," she said.

"Girls?" I asked.

"And guys," Susanna admitted. "A boy picked her up."

"Oh. Okay." I fought down the red fog of jealousy that threatened to clog my nostrils and cloud my vision.

There was nothing for me to do but wait for her, since I had to rely on Poncho for a ride home. When Martina finally showed up, she apologized for not being at the apartment to greet me, and said she'd gone to the lake "with some friends."

There was no mention of any other guys, and I didn't ask her about them. I didn't want to know the truth if she was cheating on me.

Back in Mexico City, I was lonelier than I'd ever been in my life. There were no more parties. No more friends to hang with in the bars at night. I was accustomed to laughter and teasing and the company of my noisy friends and brothers. I'd never had to sleep alone and didn't much like it. Little did I know that this time in my life would be good training for the hardships I would endure later.

■ ■ ■

Eventually, it was time for me to say goodbye to Martina for real. Poncho and I made one last trip to Guadalajara to see her and Susanna, and the girls drove us to the airport in Poncho's truck. Poncho would be staying in the United States only a short time, but I'd remain indefinitely to learn how to make American cheeses at the Klondike factory in Monroe, Wisconsin, and teach Don Poncho's workers when I returned to Mexico.

"Don't give up on me, please," I begged Martina. "I'll send for you as soon as I have money. I love you."

"I'm saving myself for you. I love you too," she said and kissed me.

We clung tightly to each other in the airport until Poncho said we had to run to make the plane.

It wasn't the first time I'd been on a plane, but it was the longest flight I'd ever taken and my first international journey. My stomach was in my throat as we took off. I stared hard through the window, imagining Martina waving to me, then sank back in exhaustion and fell asleep.

27

Desire More

Compared to the tiny terminal in Guadalajara, Chicago's O'Hare airport felt like a city within itself. Despite its size, the customs officials were well organized and courteous, and Poncho and I sailed through. Everyone in the United States really did appear to be handsome, just like in the movies. I stood out in Mexico because of my height, which was just over six feet, and my light skin and blue eyes, but here in Chicago I looked like everyone else, except for the Black people. They were the first African Americans I'd ever seen. At first I was wary—in the movies, it seemed that Black people always had guns—but they were as friendly and well dressed as everyone else in the airport.

Looking like an American, or at least a European, was both good and bad for me: nobody treated me like a foreigner, so I felt no discrimination. On the other hand, everyone assumed I spoke English, and the harsh staccato sentences were fired at me too rapidly for me to understand them.

Poncho spoke passable English—he'd had all of the educational advantages I lacked and had studied English at the university as part of his training as an engineer—so he managed to get us through the airport lines and out into the lobby. There we were met by Jorge Reinosa, my mother's friend and the man who'd arranged our exchange with Klondike Cheese Company. Jorge was short and pale-skinned; he had immigrated to Chicago because he had a brother who'd started a tortilla factory there.

Jorge's house was in a Chicago suburb where the streets and homes looked like something out of a Disney movie. The streets were nicely paved and free of trash, unlike in Guanajuato, and the cars all appeared to be new. It was June and raining lightly when we pulled into his driveway. I'd never seen so much green grass. Every lawn looked like a golf course. How, I wondered, did everyone here earn so much money? I wished Martina could see it all with me. We'd been apart less than a day, but already my heart ached for her.

The next morning, Jorge took us out to Klondike in the truck he used to pick up and deliver cheese. Poncho, still hung over from drinking the night before, fell asleep almost as soon as we hit the highway to Wisconsin. Jorge winked at me and reached into a cooler beneath the seat. He took out two glass bottles, uncapped them with his free hand, and handed one to me.

I took a thirsty gulp from the bottle and nearly gagged. Beer! I'd never seen beer in a glass bottle like this one! I'd been expecting soda. "Isn't it illegal to drink and drive here in the United States?" I asked.

Jorge put a finger to his lips. "Only if the *policia* catch you, Miguel."

Before long, we crossed the border from Illinois into Wisconsin. The countryside looked nearly the same: endless rolling fields of green corn and yellow wheat, interspersed here and there by tidy looking farms. I admired the enormous, efficient looking tractors and irrigators moving through the fields. This was a far cry from the small, often rundown family farms around Irapuato.

As we drove, Jorge told me about Wisconsin and the Klond-ike Cheese Company. "Wisconsin is *queso* country," he began, and explained that the state's first immigrants were from Switzerland in the mid-nineteenth century. Within a century the state had more than 1,500 cheese factories as other European immigrants began establishing dairy farms and producing cheese, passing down skills from generation to generation.

"Don't be surprised if you go into town and see Swiss flags still hanging up in places," he added. "And you should know that Wisconsin has been the largest queso-producing state in the United States since 1910."

The lush countryside and prosperous farms we passed lived up to the high expectations I'd formed after growing up on American television shows and movies, but my real shock came when we arrived at the Klondike Cheese Company. I literally felt my jaw drop as we toured the factory. Every piece of equipment seemed to be made of gleaming stainless steel. I might as well have been inside a space station. The floors gleamed, too. The workers all wore knee-high rubber boots and gloves and went about their jobs with brisk, no-nonsense movements. La Blanquita, which I'd thought of as grand compared to Don Vicente's tiny cojita cheese-making operation, was shabby and small by comparison to Klondike, which to me might as well have been a castle.

My heart hammered in my chest as insecurity took hold. How the hell was I ever going to teach these Americans anything about making Mexican cheese, when it was obvious they already knew so much more about cheese making than I did?

The tour continued, and eventually Jorge introduced me to the factory owners. They told me a bit about the company's history, which Jorge and Poncho translated for me as we continued walking around. The history of Klondike was also a history of the Buholzer family. Like so many other families in Wisconsin, the Buholzers had immigrated from Switzerland in the 1920s. Ernest and Marie Buholzer made Swiss cheese, and their son Alvin took up the business 20 years later.

Al and his wife, Rosa, had passed their cheese-making operation down to the men running Klondike when I arrived: their sons Ron, Dave, and Steve. The brothers had formed a family corporation when they purchased the Klondike Cheese Factory in 1972 and changed the name to Klondike Cheese Company. They had all achieved Wisconsin Master Cheesemaker® status by completing an advanced training program—the only one of its kind in the United States at that time.

Ron, Dave, and Steve were pale and dark-haired. They looked related, but Steve was taller than the other two and had curlier hair. Ron was short and heavyset, and Dave had a mustache he occasionally stroked with a finger, like it was a little pet. Dave handled most of the office business and logistics, while Steve and Ron were more hands-on in the factory. I respected them because it was clear they were the children of immigrants like me, determined to work hard and be productive.

The Buholzer brothers greeted me with smiles and handshakes and tried to make me feel at home. The more I saw of the factory, though, the more my fear settled in, bowing my shoulders as I trudged along after my guides. Eventually I shut down mentally because the English was too difficult for me to follow. What purpose could I possibly serve at Klondike? I was expected to teach them La Blanquita's way of making queso fresco, crema, and Oaxaca cheese, but operating Klondike's high-tech equipment with all of these dials and pipes and levers was beyond my abilities. I knew nothing, compared to these men.

You're going to fail at this, just like you always failed at school, I thought miserably.

No. I couldn't let that happen. Failing at this job meant I wouldn't only be failing myself, but Martina, too. Somehow I had to take this opportunity to learn something new and succeed. I picked up my head and nodded at something Ron was saying, despite not understanding a word.

■ ■ ■

Poncho was in Monroe with me for a week before he had to return to Mexico. Whenever he wasn't translating for me, the English seemed to fly at me like gravel under truck tires. I relied on my powers of observation to learn, standing silently by and watching the factory workers closely, trying to memorize their motions.

On our off hours, we drank. There wasn't much else to do in town, despite the confluence of cheese factories in and around Monroe. These included Klondike, the Chalet Cheese Co-op, Meyer Farmstead Cheese, the Swiss Colony, Roth Käse U.S.A., Grande Cheese, Henning's Cheese, Monticello Northside Swiss Cheese, and more.

There also wasn't anything to remind me of home. Nothing I ate or smelled or saw seemed familiar. The alien surroundings added to my disorientation and misery. Yes, I looked like many of these tall, blue-eyed European immigrants, but I was a poorly educated Mexican teenager who'd never before been away from home. Today, Mexicans are the largest Spanish-speaking group in Wisconsin, but back then, Poncho and I were the only Mexicans in Monroe. In fact, the only other Spanish-speaker I would meet in the months to come would be a doctor from Venezuela who was kind enough to give me a jacket when he saw me shivering in the cold. I was a lonely castaway on a sea of European immigrants.

Ron had loaned Poncho a truck so we could commute between the motel and the factory. Klondike had its own bar, the Junction House, and the men gathered there after work. I couldn't keep up with the nightly beer pounding, but I had to go wherever Poncho went if I wanted to understand anything.

One night, we left the bar with Poncho behind the wheel and ran a stop sign before Poncho slammed on the brakes. We were in Ron's truck when we stalled in the intersection. At that same moment, a motorcyclist roared toward us. The driver hit the brakes in time to avoid crashing into our truck, but the bike skidded and the driver hit the ground.

Terrified of any interactions with the local cops, Poncho floored the truck and took off the minute we saw the motorcyclist stand up and knew he was okay. The police caught up with us and tried to talk to us about the accident so they could file a report. Fortunately, this was one of the few nights Poncho hadn't been drinking to excess. The cops let us go once they saw we were driving a truck belonging to one of the Klondike owners. I suppose this was because Klondike was one of the biggest games in town. After that accident, I never let myself get drunk again.

■ ■ ■

The House that Cheese Built

Before Poncho left to fly back to Mexico, he bought Susanna gifts from the United States. I hated the idea of him arriving in Guadalajara with nothing nice for Martina, too, so I went to one of the only stores in Monroe and bought her a white faux leather jacket with red trim. The jacket cost nearly all of the money I had left—about $75—but I begged Poncho to take it back with him and give it to her.

"I need Martina to know that I love her, and I'm going to keep my promise to bring her here," I said.

"Sure, man," Poncho said, and clapped me on the shoulder. "*Buena suerte.*"

He drove me to Klondike the next morning, where we said good-bye between the factory's cheese vats. It wasn't until Poncho was actually leaving that it hit me: I had nothing more than the few clothes in my battered suitcase. I literally had no money in my pocket, no English skills, and no place to stay. I felt so scared that I nearly burst into tears as Poncho walked away, wishing for the thousandth time that I'd grown up with a father to support me, or at least one who loved and believed in me, the way Don Poncho had always been there for Poncho. Young people spin without direction when there's nobody to mentor them or support them. Now I really was a stranger in a strange land, stranded in a place where I didn't speak the language or know the customs. Home had never felt so far away.

What could I do but go to work? It was five o'clock in the morning when Poncho left. Jorge Reinosa had provided me with a fake Social Security number, which, as instructed, I gave to Thea, Steve's pretty blonde wife, who handled the payroll. She wrote down my hourly pay—$3.75/hour, much less than what the other workers were earning, though I didn't know it at the time. Not that I would have complained even if I *had* known. What could I have done? I didn't have any money or any other place to go. I was stranded. Shipwrecked. A prisoner of my own choices.

Thea used sign language to demonstrate how to punch my time card in the machine. A rough looking guy on the factory line showed me how to do my sweaty, back-breaking, tedious first job at Klondike: take 40-pound blocks of cheese and use a sharp cutter to slice it into 1-pound blocks. For the next 16 hours, I cut block after block of cheddar and Monterrey jack cheese in the hot, humid air.

The factory never stopped. I worked like a robot, sweat streaming down my forehead and darkening my shirt. They'd given me a pair of knee-high rubber boots like the rest of the employees wore, so my feet were perspiring, too. It felt like I was wading through puddles of my own sweat.

At last someone realized I hadn't taken a break and pulled me aside, gesturing toward the room where the workers gathered to eat meals and drink coffee. Most brought their food from home or bought it from the vending machines. My limbs were shaking with fatigue, and my stomach churned with hunger. I'd spent all of my money on Martina's jacket; I turned my pockets inside out and found a handful of loose coins, nothing more.

Then I spotted a loaf of bread on the counter and a block of cheese. I hastily made a cheese sandwich, glancing over my shoulder in panic as I microwaved it to make the cheese melt, wondering if I was stealing someone else's food. But I was desperate. I'd never been so homesick for Mexican food and my mother's cooking and company as I was that day, while chewing through the gluey cheddar cheese sandwiched between tasteless white bread, washing it down with water I guzzled from the sink.

By the end of my first shift, my neck and shoulder muscles felt like they were on fire from repeating the same lifting and slicing motions all day long. I thought I'd worked hard at Don Poncho's, but that was nothing compared to the way people labored in the United States. At Klondike, they stopped only for brief breaks. We were processing up to 32 vats of cheese daily—twice the amount we processed at La Blanquita—but there was no lounging about or long breaks for tortas and cold drinks. During one of my breaks, I was so exhausted that I fell asleep standing up against the wall in the bathroom.

But I had another, more pressing problem than aching muscles. While Poncho was here, I'd been sleeping in his motel room, but now what? I had no place to stay. I didn't know a soul, and I didn't speak English well enough to ask if I could crash at somebody's house. I had never felt so alone.

I waited for the shift to file out of the factory, the men hollering at one another as they climbed into their vehicles—mostly pickup trucks—and roared out of the parking lot. When I was alone, I searched the factory, worn suitcase in hand, for a place I could sleep undetected, and discovered the boiler room. It was clean, at least, and separated from the rest of the factory. The rolling metal door was never locked, and when I pulled it shut, I was protected from the weather.

Inside the boiler room, there was a well-equipped workshop on the left, a room with tools hanging from the walls, giant saws, grinders, pipes, and several worktables. On the right side of the room was nothing but a flat wall with pipes running up it. I found some flattened pieces of cardboard and dragged them over to this part of the boiler room. Then I curled up in my clothes and lost consciousness, too tired to cry, depression seated like a giant black dog on my chest, making it difficult to breathe.

■ ■ ■

The next day, I rose early and washed in the men's room, then lived that hell all over again. I could barely read and write in Spanish, given my dyslexia and attention issues in school; to get by, I had to observe everything and everyone carefully and create my own narrative of what was happening. I did this even when I was small and the teachers asked us to answer questions about a lesson, pretending to read and making up the answers because I didn't want the other children to laugh at me for not knowing how to read.

Now, my early training in observing others allowed me to pay close attention to everything with my hands, ears, and eyes as I worked at Klondike. "Listen and keep *your boca shut*," I reminded myself several times daily, while people gave me directions and showed me what to do. Fortunately it was the same routine at first, day in, day out, cutting up those huge blocks of cheese.

In the evenings I retreated to my cardboard bed in the boiler room, sore and exhausted, and woke with stiff limbs, my belly growling with hunger. This might have been my life for a long time, if Ron's son hadn't spotted me sneaking into the boiler room after a few days and outed me to the bosses.

Ron pulled me aside after work that day and drove me to the Junction House. There, he introduced me to Dave Jacobs, the bartender. Ron told him about my predicament, and Dave invited me to stay in his apartment above the bar. When Ron realized I didn't have any money—this, too, I had to demonstrate, turning my pockets inside out for him and shrugging, which made him laugh—he gave me an advance of $25 on my paycheck so I could pay Dave some rent money and buy food.

The apartment was small, but clean and comfortable. I even had my own bedroom. Dave and I couldn't really communicate, since he spoke no Spanish and my English was nearly nonexistent, but he was a nice guy. He adored his Harley Davidson and disappeared on his motorcycle for a few days every week, leaving me on my own.

With so many empty, solitary hours, I sank deeper and deeper into depression. My days began at 5 a.m. and didn't end until 6 p.m. I managed to phone Martina several times from the factory before Thea noticed the bills and warned me not to do it again. Each phone call cost nearly as much as I earned in a day! Without being able to hear Martina's voice, talk to anyone in my family, or communicate with anyone else in Spanish, I felt completely isolated. Who would even know if I got sick or died?

Even buying food was problematic. The nearest grocery store was 7 miles away, and I didn't have a car. Walking to the store wasn't bad in the summer months, but as the days turned colder and shorter, I'd get home from the factory after work and find myself having to walk in the dark. Many days I ate nothing more than mustard and onion sandwiches or banana hot dogs—bananas tucked into slices of bread.

One night, I was coming home with a small bag of food from the corner store—canned food, bags of chips, and other junk—when a motorcycle rumbled up to me. I barely had time to turn around before I felt something hard hit me in the head. Then the motorcyclist was off his bike and on top of me, punching my face and stomach until I passed out on the sidewalk.

An hour later, I regained consciousness, bloody and bruised, and stumbled around, collecting my groceries and carrying them under my arms because the bag had split. At the apartment, I iced my face and thought about the attack. The man hadn't taken anything, not even the food on the ground. Clearly he wasn't a thief. So why had he gone after me like that? Was it because I was Mexican? Could he somehow tell I was different?

Then it dawned on me: this motorcyclist was probably the one Poncho and I had nearly crashed into our first week here. This was payback. Somehow that made me feel better than if it had been a random attack.

Another night, the guys at the factory invited me to go drinking. It was December by then and starting to snow. I was glad the Venezuelan doctor had taken pity on me and given me a warm coat as we crunched across the parking lot to one of the pickup trucks and climbed inside. We drove to a bar farther from work, and I laughed at jokes I didn't understand from my place in the back seat, pleased to think I was making friends even though I couldn't comprehend most of what they said.

We drank for a while and played some pool. As usual, I couldn't keep up with them. These men seemed to work just so they could afford to go to the bar and drink up their paychecks. I couldn't handle the same amount of liquor they could. Nor did I want to: I badly needed every cent I made, and I couldn't afford to lose my job. They could come in late or drunk, get fired, and find another job easily. It wouldn't be that easy for me.

Finally it was last call and time to leave. On our way back to the factory, the driver suddenly stopped the truck on a dark road. "Get out of the car, Miguel," he ordered.

"*¿Que chingados?*" I looked out the window and saw only black sky above fields frosted white. I had no idea where we were. The other guys started laughing and everyone began shoving me toward the door.

"Come on, Miguel, end of the line, buddy!" one said. "This is your stop."

"Time to walk off those beers," another said, and climbed out of the truck to hold the door open for me. "Out, you fucking Mexican!"

Everyone was laughing except me as I nearly fell out of the truck, terrified they might beat me up like the motorcyclist had. I'd be finished, out here in the cold and the dark, if they did that.

But the truck roared off. I started walking home, feeling the cruel bite of snow on my face and through the thin soles of my shoes, wishing I had worn a hat, at least. My only hope was that, if I walked long enough, maybe I'd find a gas station with an unlocked restroom, or a barn, where I could camp out until morning. Tears ran down my face. I thought of Martina, of Mexico's sunbaked streets, of my mother and brothers. I was so cold and alone. What was I doing in this country?

The pain of that moment brought back another time when I'd been hurt and betrayed, another unwanted memory of my father. I was probably nine or ten years old, and my father had started drinking early in the day and fighting with my mother. He'd locked me out of the house, but through the kitchen window, I could see my father holding my mother against the wall by the hair and hitting her. Without hesitation, I had kicked the door to get his attention. Who knows what gave me the courage? But I was seized by a raw animal fury.

"Why are you picking on Mama?" I had yelled. "Let her go, you son of a bitch! If you're a man, you'll let her go and fight me instead!" My voice was still high, a child's voice, but I kept kicking the door and yelling at him. "You want a fight? Come and get me! I'll give you a fight!"

My father had finally opened the door. "You little bastard!" he roared. "Don't you speak to me that way! I'll kill you, talking like that to your old man!"

I took off at a run. He followed me out of the house and down the narrow cobbled street, surprisingly fast. I was terrified, but still I kept taunting him, leading him farther and farther away from the house and my sobbing mother.

"Fuck you, asshole. Leave my mother alone. Come and beat me if you can catch me!" I screamed, loud enough for everyone on the street to hear us. People were looking out their windows, but nobody dared to intervene when my father was on the warpath. He was The Transformer. Unstoppable. Invincible.

I kept running blindly through the streets, certain he'd kill me if he caught me. At last I had flung myself through the doors of a church and crawled beneath the altar. When I saw my father hesitate in the doorway, I bit my finger to avoid crying out in terror.

He didn't have the courage to come into the church and haul me out of there. After a few minutes, my father disappeared. I stayed there on the icy stone floor in the dark, trembling with cold and fear, wondering what he was doing to my poor mother, until the priest found me.

"You have to leave, son," he said. "You can't stay here."

I was too frightened and angry to return home. Instead, I fled to my friend Eladio's house and pleaded with him to let me stay. "Please, help me out," I cried. "My dad is crazy. If I go back, he'll kill me."

I stayed there a week, then went to my friend Octavio's house, returning home only when I knew my father wasn't there or wasn't drinking.

My father was a cruel bastard, but he was a fact of life, one who had made me distrust everyone. I never could fully trust my brothers, either, because there was always the possibility that they might leave me behind or beat me up. I certainly couldn't trust my mother to protect me. Martina was the only person in my life who truly made me feel loved and secure.

Headlights came around a corner suddenly, blinding me, and a truck rumbled to a stop, filled with laughing, hooting men. I nearly ran for my life in terror. Then I recognized the driver: it was the same truck I'd ridden in when I left the Klondike factory hours ago.

"Get in, Miguel!" the driver called.

"Yeah, we were only fucking with you, man," another guy called from the back seat.

"No, *gracias*," I said, waving them off. "I think I'll walk."

"Shit, don't be stupid. It was just a joke, Miguel," said a third guy. "We were just messing around. No need to look at us like that."

Like what? I wondered, pretending to laugh. "Nah, I'm good. I'll walk. I need to clear my *cabeza*."

"Come on," the driver said, and finally I relented. But when I recognized the stop sign near my street, I told them to stop and got out. Clearly, the only one I could trust here was myself.

They took off again, leaving me alone on that dark icy road.

The House that Cheese Built

There were many times like this during those first dark months in the United States when I despaired of ever understanding this American culture, which was so different from what I'd grown up seeing on TV and in the movies. However, my isolation served me, in a way, because it forced me to pay close attention to what everyone did around me. Even if you're doing a job so low on the totem pole that nobody else wants it—the sorts of jobs immigrants in this country often end up doing—pay attention to every detail, even when you think it doesn't matter.

Don't just show up, do the bare minimum, and collect your paycheck. Ask questions and ask for more responsibility. That way, when new opportunities knock on your door, you'll have the knowledge to take advantage of them.

Little did I know it, but during these dark hours I was acquiring a good work ethic and the skills I needed to be a trustworthy employee. This would lead me toward being valued by the company and, eventually, to creating cheeses that would turn the American cheese industry on its head.

Chapter 3

Create Opportunity

**People Say Look for New Business
Opportunities. I Say Create Your Own.**

Imagine being in a place where you can't understand what people are saying, the food is foreign, the customs are strange, and you're always looking over your shoulder because you can't trust anyone. I was taking classes in the University of Life, and it felt like I was in prison. Ironically, this would be good training for when I really did have to spend time in prison many years later.

During those early months in Monroe, I tried to escape twice. My loneliness was so sharply acute that it drove me to pack my few pathetic belongings into my suitcase and start walking toward the bus station in the dead of winter, crying so hard I could barely see. Both times, though, I had no choice but to turn around. I couldn't afford a bus ticket, much less plane fare to Mexico. I was truly stuck, more or less an indentured servant.

Some nights, I couldn't stop weeping. My 20th birthday came and went, and I was alone in a way I'd never been alone before. The jobs they gave me at the factory continued to be back-breakingly difficult. Working in the cheese factory was like slaving in some giant's kitchen: it was hot, noisy, and damp, and you were constantly on your feet and in motion. Muscles ached in places I didn't even know I *had* muscles. The factory was smelly too; even after a shower, I stank like sour milk.

What drove me to keep putting one foot in front of the other were the letters and cassette tapes Martina mailed me. Her letters let me hear her voice and feel her arms around me. I was doing this for Martina, I reminded myself. For *us*. Life had handed me this destiny, and I was going to make the most of it so we'd have a better future. Work was all I had, so I threw myself into it, day after day after day, becoming a sponge for knowledge.

■ ■ ■

Here's the thing: you can't give up on yourself because only your tenacity will get you through the hard times. My determination had already saved me from my father's beatings and from drowning when my father threw me in the water. Now it would save me from failing at the first real opportunity I'd ever had to make something of myself.

When I asked for extra hours, the owners at Klondike put me to work scrubbing floors and paid me to wash their cars and trucks. I did all of this without complaining. A few months into the job, Klondike moved me along the factory line, from cutting cheese blocks to washing the thick plastic tubes that had little holes for squeezing the cheese through the pipes. As I took the pieces apart and scrubbed them clean, I continued observing the other workers and memorized how they operated the machines, literally following the pieces of equipment with my eyes, or sometimes with my hands, trying to understand how the machines were put together and how they functioned.

The work at Klondike took more discipline than anything I'd ever done in my life. Starting with the milk being processed and ending with the cheese being cut into blocks and wrapped for retailers, everything in between had to be done at a certain pace and with no variations in the routines. If the workers didn't follow the cheese recipes step by step, with exacting precision, the product might turn out to be something different or even be ruined completely. Quality mattered to the Buholzers. The workers couldn't ever take random breaks just because they were tired. They drank hard, but they worked even harder. I'd never seen such discipline. I didn't always like these men, but I admired them. What's more, I knew I had to work hard enough to keep up, or Klondike might replace me.

After a few months, I became more at ease with the rhythms of the factory and secretly chose a mentor: David Webster. It was clear that the owners of Klondike relied on him. If a machine had a problem, Webster—everyone called him that—could usually fix whatever it was without calling Steve or Ron to help him; he'd rather handle problems himself than bother anyone else.

Webster was a skilled cheesemaker and head of the whole show at Klondike. He was a bighearted guy, loyal and responsible at work. He drank very little and was sometimes too quiet, but these particular qualities made me trust him even more. He was Nordic looking, as tall and blue-eyed as I was, but with blond hair. He was a few years older, probably already in his mid-20s, and already married. He started his work shift at midnight and controlled every step of the operations. I made it my mission to shadow him any chance I could.

As my English improved, I began asking Webster questions about the factory and why things were done the way they were. He patiently explained every process and seemed to appreciate my keen interest and enthusiasm. In return, I embraced the opportunity to make top quality cheese.

Within a year, Webster and I were communicating well enough that we became friends. I learned that he had grown up on a dairy farm next to Klondike, and his family sold milk to the factory. Webster had known the Buholzer brothers since they were children. It was easy for him to walk across the street from his house to work at the factory, so that's what he'd been doing since adolescence.

As I got to know Webster better, he invited me to his family farm occasionally, where I helped them bale hay and had pancakes with maple syrup for the first time. They offered to pay me, but even as poor as I was, I couldn't take their money. I considered them friends and was happy to help. The only sore spot between Webster and me was his wife; she was a sour, closed sort of person and made it clear she thought I was beneath them.

When Webster and I were alone, he was still quiet, even taciturn. I did my best to get him to talk. One day we were driving a truck for Klondike and Webster barely spoke, no matter how much I pestered him with questions or told him jokes.

Eventually we stopped for gas, and he said, "Bring me a quart of ice cream, will you?"

"Sure." I hopped out of the cab, bought the ice cream, and returned. Webster finished pumping the diesel and climbed back in behind the wheel without even saying thank you.

He liked to take off his rubber boots while he drove because his feet got too hot; I was peeved enough by my friend's stubborn silence that I took one of the boots and hid it. The next time we stopped for gas, Webster started looking around for his boot. When he didn't find it, he still said nothing, only got out of the truck to fill the tank and take a leak. When he came back, he threw his remaining boot into the trash.

"Why are you throwing that *bota* away?" I asked, biting back a laugh.

"I lost the other one," he said with a grunt.

"You never asked me where it was, did you?" I produced the boot from under the seat.

"You son of a bitch," he said, but then we were both laughing.

It wasn't long before Webster asked Steve to make me his secondhand guy. We started sharing responsibilities more equally, with me coming into the factory at 2:30 a.m. to help him start up the machines and get the day's processes going before the morning shift workers arrived.

Little did I know it then, but by focusing on learning from Webster and mastering the craft of making cheese at Klondike, I was preparing to build my own cheese empire one day.

■ ■ ■

After a few months, Dave Jacobs asked me to move out of his apartment so his girlfriend could move in. For a time I lived in the basement of a friend of his, a redheaded woman named Merry who had two kids and was going through a complicated divorce. She and I seldom saw each other because I had to leave at two or three o'clock most mornings to go to the factory. When Merry moved to Milwaukee for a better job, I found a small apartment of my own.

Not long after that, a new guy showed up at work. Jeff had been hired by Klondike years before, straight out of high school. He'd been sent to prison for fighting in a bar and had lost his driver's license due to drunk driving. Now he was on parole.

"Hey, Miguel," Steve asked a few days after Jeff showed up. "Any chance Jeff could stay with you for a while? He needs help getting back on his feet."

"Of course." I was happy to have a roommate—the nights were still far too lonely—and I was also glad to offer a helping hand to someone in need, just like Steve and his brothers had done for me.

Jeff was about 10 years older than I was, a short, bulky guy with straight brown hair and a round face. He was an amiable roommate, though he drank to the point of blacking out many nights. We rubbed along fairly peacefully until the day Steve called me into his office.

"Listen, Miguel, Webster's got to take some time off work," he said. "We'd like you to assume his position while he's out. Think you can handle that?"

"I can," I said eagerly, proud that Steve had noticed my hard work.

That night, I went into work at midnight to start up the machines and begin Klondike's processing for the next day. I was a little nervous, but I did these tasks easily. I'd been working alongside Webster for a few months, and I'd memorized every pipe, tube, switch, valve, and operational step. I didn't need the written instructions Webster had left; in fact, I wouldn't have been able to read them in English anyway. My conversational English was becoming more fluent, but between my dyslexia and poor literacy skills in Spanish, learning to read English seemed like a Herculean task. The strange words swam together whenever I saw them written down.

Steve clapped me on the back the next morning when he saw everything was up and running as it should be. "Good job," he said.

That night, however, I was dead asleep in my bed when suddenly I felt the sharp edge of a knife at my throat. My eyes flew open. Jeff was in my room; he'd pinned me down on the bed, his face red with rage and his breath sour with the smell of whatever he'd been drinking.

"You fucking son of a Mexican whore," Jeff slurred. "I'm going to fucking end you!"

I froze, reduced to the small, frightened boy I'd been around my father whenever he was raging drunk and looking for a place to land his fists. "*¿Que pasa?*" I managed, scrambling away from the knife. "What the hell is wrong with you, Jeff?"

"YOU, that's what's fucking wrong with me!" Jeff shouted, spittle hitting my face.

"What did I ever do to you?" I tried maintaining eye contact even as he waved the knife around in my face. "Look, whatever's eating you, let's talk about it. *Calmate pendejo.*"

"You took my job!" Jeff shoved me in the chest. "It should have been *me* working Webster's shift. Why the fuck did they promote some Mexican *wetback* over *me*?"

The House that Cheese Built

I lost it and shoved him back so that Jeff stumbled away. I remained in the bedroom, feet planted on the floor, terrified that he might come back and attack me again, but pretty soon there was the smell of cigarette smoke from the kitchen and the clink of another beer bottle being opened. If I was lucky, he'd pass out at the table.

I waited until things were quiet, then dressed and left for the factory, passing Jeff in the kitchen. He was seated with his forehead resting on the kitchen table, a cigarette smoldering in an ashtray full of butts. When I told Steve what had happened, he immediately fired Jeff. I gave Jeff back his rent money after he'd shoved his few belongings into a bag, still muttering things about Mexicans stealing jobs.

■ ■ ■

Bit by bit, I became a better cheesemaker. I also began dreaming of bigger opportunities. After I'd been working alongside Webster for about a year, I turned to him after one fatiguing shift and said, "Do you ever want more out of life than this?"

He gave me his usual enigmatic shrug. "Like what, man?"

It occurred to me that, although Webster was well respected by Klondike's owners and was an expert cheesemaker, he'd seen little of the world. He'd done nothing in his life but work on his family's farm next door and Klondike. He'd been at the factory for 15 years, was already married, and had a child. He was clearly averse to taking risks. Despite the gaps in my education and my halting English, I'd already learned a lot about how to navigate the world and the many different kinds of people in it.

By sending me to the United States, Don Poncho had granted me a huge opportunity, but I desperately wanted to expand my career options and earn more money. I even dreamed of being in business for myself. As early as age six, I'd been an entrepreneur, taking a shoeshine kit into the plaza and knocking on doors to offer my services, working for a few centavos a day. In middle school, I had cleaned parts at an agricultural machine parts factory, proud to hand my earnings over to my mother, who took in boarding school students to make ends meet.

At age 15, I had helped my father deliver bottled drinking water to customers. This was a good business model: his partner, Ricardo, passed well water through a filter and bottled it himself, so the profit on a 20-liter bottle was decent. My father and I went door to door, selling the bottled water whenever he was sober enough to drive the truck. Sometimes I drove the truck when he wasn't. Eventually, Ricardo got sick of dealing with my father's bullshit and blew up the business. My father went off to sell cemetery plots next, and I began peddling jeans at the flea market for my brother Carlos, who'd started a jeans factory with my grandfather's help.

Now I had an idea for a business—my own business. I had learned a great deal about cheese making. At the same time, I'd been missing Mexican food. Jorge Reinosa, my mother's friend in Chicago, had told me about the Mexican immigrants living in and around Rockford, Illinois. If I was homesick for the taste of Mexico, they must be, too. What if we could tap into that market and sell Mexican-style cheese?

"Webster," I said slowly, "I have an idea, and I want you to hear me out before you react, okay?"

This wasn't a problem for Webster. He was always a good listener. The two of us were similar in that way. He gave me that one-shouldered shrug and nodded. "Okay."

I took a deep breath and said, "We should make *queso* for Mexican immigrants and sell it to them directly. What if Steve and Ron let us use the machines on weekends when the factory's closed?"

"Huh," Webster said. "Interesting." His hands continued to robotically work the valves and dials of the machine he was operating. "Let me think on it."

Even as young and impatient as I was, I knew better than to push him. This was why I trusted Webster: he gave every idea serious consideration before making up his mind. That's why we were such a good pair; I was impulsive enough to take risks, but he was careful about assessing them. I could push him forward while he kept us from potentially making a drastic mistake.

The next morning, Webster agreed my idea had "potential." We went to Steve, Dave, and Ron, who readily agreed to let us use the factory on weekends to make our own cheese as long as we paid for whatever milk we used.

"Who knows? Maybe you'll help us break into the Hispanic cheese market," Ron said.

■ ■ ■

We decided that muenster cheese would be the easiest to produce and the most marketable. We had all of the equipment and ingredients for the muenster recipe at Klondike already. This soft, creamy cow's milk cheese was similar to what most Mexicans and other Latinx immigrants used in quesadillas. Naturally we called it "La Martina"; Martina even helped us design a label.

Webster and I worked all day Saturday, making the muenster one batch at a time. It took forever to make the cheese and cut it into blocks with only two of us on the job. On Sunday, we wrapped the cheese and packed it into boxes we kept in the cooler. Monday we started our usual workweek, and the following Saturday we drove to Rockford with our first batch of cheese in a refrigerated truck.

Finding places to sell La Martina cheese was easy: we simply looked in the yellow pages of the phone book for stores specializing in goods from Mexico and other places in Latin America. The store owners really wanted to buy our cheese—there was literally no Hispanic-style cheese on the market in Wisconsin at that time—and they quickly bought everything we had. Webster and I were so ecstatic that we spent all of our profits on beer and pizza.

This grueling regime lasted a few weeks, until we were so exhausted that one day we fell asleep by the side of the road in Rockford after having sold a new batch of cheese out of our truck. A Black guy rapped on the driver's side window and woke me.

"Hey, man, I thought you were dead," the guy said, and sauntered away, his hands deep in his pockets.

I rubbed my face. I might as well have been dead. My limbs felt like rubber and my back ached like somebody had driven a spike through it. "Webster," I said, nudging him awake. "It's time to go home."

He had been slumped against the window; now Webster roused himself and turned to look at me, his eyes huge and owl-like as he swiveled his head in my direction. "Man, I feel like I was run over by a truck."

I nodded. "We can't keep up this pace."

"Nope," he said, and that was it, the end of our first business venture.

■ ■ ■

Successful entrepreneurs the world over have one thing in common: they keep testing new ideas until they find one that flies. When Webster told me a few months later that the US government had declared that the separators—the machines used to separate cream from whole milk—no longer met US standards for safe machinery and were being replaced by machines that were more automated, I was stunned. To me, the separators we'd been using were much safer and more efficient than anything I'd seen in Mexican cheese operations.

"What will they do with the old machines?" I asked Webster.

He shrugged. "Don't know. Toss 'em, probably."

How could you throw out perfectly good equipment? I couldn't get over that. In Mexico, if you had an accident with your bicycle and twisted the rim and spokes, you could find bike mechanics on nearly every corner who would twist your wheel back into shape, and people regularly combed the dumps for goods they could sell or use themselves. Just throwing out perfectly good, expensive machinery, which up until yesterday had served this very factory, rubbed me the wrong way.

The more I thought about this, the more I wondered if there were a business opportunity here—one that might be easier than making cheese on my own. There were 375 cheese factories in our area alone that were about to unload useful equipment.

Before long I was on the phone with Poncho, my friend at La Blanquita, telling him what was going on. "Hey, can you sell some separators in *México* if I send them down to you?" I asked.

"*Claro*," he said, and we quickly worked out a deal: I'd receive $5,000 for every separator I could get to the border. He'd sell them to Mexican factories for $6,000 and keep the profit.

I needed a partner, someone who knew the people in the cheese factories and who spoke English well enough to bargain with them for their separators. I decided to approach Webster. He and Kevin Weiss, another friend I'd made at Klondike, were still the only two people I really trusted in the United States.

"Listen," I told Webster, "there's a guy in *México* who wants to buy some of those separators Klondike and other factories are dumping. Want to help me sell them?"

As always, Webster listened carefully. Then he nodded. "Seems like easy money," he said.

It was. We picked up discarded separators at little or no cost, because the US factories were eager to get rid of them and avoid paying fines to the government. Webster and I rented a flatbed truck and drove the machines to the Mexican border, two at a time, where

Poncho met us and transported the machines to sell to factories in Mexico. Because this was agricultural equipment, we didn't have to pay taxes.

It was a win-win: Webster and I were helping the cheese factories in Wisconsin recycle old equipment. At the same time, we were helping to modernize the Mexican dairy industry and making a quick profit. Even after splitting the money 50/50, I netted $25,000 in less than a year.

Best of all? Before this, I was dying a slow death, doing the same dead-end jobs at Klondike for such a low wage that I could scarcely save any money. Now I had enough cash to bring Martina to the United States and marry her.

I'd managed to fly home to see Martina twice during my first 18 months in the United States. On my second trip, I was on my way back from Poncho's wedding when I was picked up by immigration authorities in the Houston airport because I'd been stupid enough to only buy a one-way ticket. They deported me back to Mexico City on a plane that was so full I had to sit in the toilets after a cop warned the flight attendants to watch me, like I was a criminal.

I bought a round-trip ticket for Martina from Guadalajara so the immigration officials wouldn't suspect her of wanting to stay permanently in the United States. Martina was as eager to come and live with me as I was to have her by my side; we were so desperate to be together that she was even willing to drop out of the university. We arranged everything by phone. A week later, I went to the airport with a bouquet of flowers to wait for her, my heart pounding so hard, I was sure everyone must be able to hear it.

This was in the pre–mobile phone era, so I had no way to communicate with Martina when she didn't arrive on her scheduled flight. *She must have missed it*, I thought, and waited for the next one. She wasn't on that plane, either. Now I was really worried. What if she'd been in a car accident on the way to the airport? It never once crossed my mind that she might have decided not to come—that's how much I loved and trusted her.

I waited at O'Hare airport in Chicago until nearly midnight, frustrated and increasingly frantic, wondering what had happened to Martina while the flowers wilted in my arms. Finally I drove to Jorge Reinosa's house—my mother's friend, the one I'd originally stayed with when Poncho and I first came to Chicago—and called Martina. I phoned her apartment first, and when Martina didn't answer, I gathered my courage and called her parents' house.

Her mother answered the phone. When I asked if Martina was there and whether everything was okay, she screamed, "How dare you fucking call our house after what you did, Miguel?"

I tried to stay calm, though I could feel my anger rising like a red tide blurring my vision. I hated that feeling. Losing my temper only reminded me of my father, and I never wanted to be that kind of man. I struggled to keep my voice calm. "Look, I'm just calling to talk to Martina. Is she there? Is she all right?"

"She's here, and yes, she's fine, no thanks to you, asshole!" Martina's mother shouted. She began insulting me right and left, telling me I was ruining her daughter's future by convincing her to run away and live in sin with me. "You're a fucking low-life bastard, Miguel," she said.

Eventually, the truth came out: Martina's sister, Alejandra, had picked up the other phone extension when Martina and I were making our plans. She'd overheard everything and immediately told their parents, who had driven straight to Guadalajara and literally caught Martina packing a suitcase in her apartment. They'd demanded that Martina go home with them, and declared they were finished paying her college tuition if all she wanted to do was ruin her life by shacking up with a ghetto dog like me.

"Martina's 21," I argued desperately, even knowing it was pointless. "She's old enough to know her own mind. You can't stop her!"

Create Opportunity

"That's what you think. Watch me!" Martina's mother yelled, and hung up.

I was gutted by the disappointment of not having Martina join me in the United States, but I was determined not to let her parents win and break us apart. Fortunately for me, their plan to keep her at home backfired. Because they'd yanked Martina out of school, made her live at home again, and refused to continue paying for her to go to any other college, she was more miserable than ever without me. We immediately began plotting another secret meeting. This time, I would come to her.

I'd been in the United States for nearly two years by then. Now, with $25,000 in the bank from selling the separators, I felt like the richest man in Wisconsin, or maybe even Mexico. In actuality, compared to most Mexicans my age, I probably *was* wealthy. According to the Borgen Project (https://borgenproject.org/poverty-in-mexico-2/), even today, around half of all Mexicans live in poverty. About 25 million Mexicans are currently earning less than $14/day. In my hometown of Irapuato, a relatively prosperous place, the police make only 1,300 pesos a week today—that's the equivalent of $63. Who can feed a family on that, much less buy gas for your car, pay rent, and save any money for retirement, or, God forbid, a medical emergency or a catastrophe like an earthquake or flood?

I had two reasons to fly home when I did. The first, obviously, was that I had been yearning to see Martina again, to hear her sweet voice and hold her in my arms. I wanted her to know that I was planning to keep my promise and make her my wife.

The second, more immediate reason to go home at that time was because my brother Pedro was getting married, though I didn't tell anyone in my family that I was going to be there. I couldn't chance having them tell Martina's family about my arrival, because Martina and I were going to meet in Guadalajara in secret before the wedding. I knew her parents would probably nail her bedroom door shut if they thought she was going to see me.

Before leaving Wisconsin, I bought new clothes, the finest I could find around Monroe, plus a new coat and hat, and a pair of shoes— the first pair I'd ever had that weren't passed down to me. Even the rubber boots I wore to work had been given to me by the Buholzer family. I was determined to arrive in Mexico looking sharp, like a man who was confident, skilled, and reliable. In short, I wanted to look like a man Martina's family would *want* her to marry.

I worried all the way to Guadalajara from Chicago, imagining showing up at the airport in Mexico and not finding Martina there. Imagining her being held prisoner by her parents because they loathed me. If that were the case, I would go and get her, I decided, even if I had to break down the door of their farmhouse. They weren't going to succeed in keeping us apart this time.

As the plane disembarked, I was toward the back of the line of passengers. I kept hopping up and down, trying to see over the crowd, my eyes searching everywhere for this woman who meant the whole world to me.

And then there she was. Martina was dressed simply, in white pants and a green sweater, but at that moment she looked more beautiful than any movie star. We hugged and danced around in our excitement like a pair of kids. We couldn't believe we were finally together! The months we'd been apart evaporated like a puddle in the Mexican sun. It seemed as if we'd always been in this embrace, this dance of joy.

We didn't let go of each other even as we walked out of the airport, and we drove straight to a hotel in Guadalajara where nobody could find us. We made love without bothering to even unpack the bags or unmake the bed. When we finished, we dozed in each other's arms, then woke up and made love again, this time more slowly, savoring every sensation.

Create Opportunity

After my brother's wedding at the Club Compestre, where my family was shocked to see me, I went to my in-laws' farm with my mother and oldest brother Joaquin to properly ask for Martina's hand in marriage. By then, my in-laws had heard I was in town and knew that Martina and I had spent the night together in a hotel. Her parents accepted my proposal—what else could they do, if they were going to save their daughter's reputation?—but made one request.

"Wait a year," Martina's mother said. I could tell by the tone of her voice that, despite my obvious financial stability, she was still trying to look down on me and my family because we were poor.

I have always judged people not according to wealth or social status, but on who they are, on their knowledge and ethics, and on how they treat others with kindness. Money didn't matter to me back then, other than wanting to have enough to provide for Martina and the family I hoped we'd have one day. Today I'm considered wealthy by most standards, but money matters to me even less. I can't tolerate people who judge others by income and social class.

But I held my temper for Martina's sake. If we were going to marry, my wife would be happier if she had her parents' approval. Martina and I agreed to wait a year before our wedding. I knew that having a year-long engagement would allow my in-laws to keep hoping that Martina would snag a rich husband before I put a ring on her finger. It would also keep tongues from wagging about how Martina must be marrying me because I'd gotten her pregnant. Preserving the family's reputation meant supporting the illusion that Martina was still a virgin, since they professed to be staunch Catholics like my own mother.

I had no engagement ring for Martina, so I made one out of a red rubber band and put it on her finger. "Wait for me, *mi amor*," I whispered, pulling her close. "You have my love and loyalty forever."

She kissed me hard. "I'll wait for you," she said. "I promise."

"Me too," I said. "There is no woman for me but you."

With those vows exchanged, I flew back to Wisconsin to spend another lonely year without Martina.

■ ■ ■

I wouldn't say the work was easier for me at Klondike, or that the nights were any less long while I waited to be with Martina, but I kept busy by trying to get the apartment ready. I owned very little, preferring instead to save all of my money, but when I looked around my empty one-bedroom apartment with nothing much in it but the bed that David Buholzer had given me when I first moved into my own place, I realized I couldn't bring Martina here without fixing things up. I put the word out to everyone I knew, and gradually people started offering me pieces of furniture and boxes of dishes and linens they had stored in their garages and attics—further proof of how much more American families had, in terms of material goods, than the average Mexican family.

Soon, my apartment looked like an actual home. My next step was to find a real ring for Martina. Fortunately for me, though less so for him, a friend of mine had just broken off his engagement. He had bought a ring with the tiniest sliver of diamond in it, maybe 1/16th of a carat, and offered to sell it to me for $200. This was still a lot of money for me, but I said yes, if he'd agree to let me pay off the ring over time.

A year later, with that ring in my pocket, I flew back to Mexico the day before my wedding. This time my brother picked me up at the airport and drove me to a place where I could rent a black tuxedo. I was 23 years old and the happiest man on the planet when my mother helped me put the cuff links through my stiff white shirt. Although I didn't think my heart could possibly be any fuller, my joy at seeing Martina walk down the aisle of the same church where my grandparents had been married—the same church where my grandmother had painted murals on the walls—was like sunlight beaming

59

Create Opportunity

over the congregation, illuminating Martina like an angel in her white wedding dress.

We spent our wedding night in the Camino Real in Guanajuato, where all of those tiny buttons that made Martina's wedding dress so elegant proved to be a frustrating task for an eager bridegroom. At last, though, we were naked and ready to make love.

There was another wedding reception taking place in the courtyard below. As I lay down beside Martina on the bed, the two of us finally naked, she pointed to the big windows overlooking the party and said, "Can you please close the curtains?"

"Sure," I said, and hopped out of bed again.

To my shock, in my eagerness to pull the curtains shut, the entire rod gave way and the curtains fell down, revealing every inch of my passion to the party below. People started laughing, and so did I, but Martina was so mortified that we called reception and asked to change rooms. We walked down the hall with blankets wrapped around us, holding hands and laughing.

The next day, in true Mexican fashion, we had a blow-out party at Martina's childhood home that started in the afternoon and finished in the early hours of the next morning. As I looked around at the boisterous crowd of friends and family members gathered from both sides, I finally felt accepted. It was as if I'd already won the game of life. Nothing could stop me from being successful and happy with Martina at my side.

We spent the three days of our honeymoon—all the vacation I could take from Klondike—in Puerto Vallarta, where I felt like my heart might burst with happiness every morning when I woke up and saw Martina's hair spread out in a fan on the pillow next to mine, and felt her warm body curled against me. We ate and drank, swam and made love, and it seemed to me that my adult life had truly begun. Martina, too, was happy, constantly reaching for my hand when we walked together, or pressing her hip and thigh against mine if we were seated, so that I'd instantly want to tear off her clothes.

When we flew back to O'Hare, we passed through customs separately to play it safe, since Martina was supposedly coming into the United States as a tourist. We made it through immigration control without incident and picked up the tiny Volkswagen Caribe I'd borrowed so I could drive Martina to Monroe in style. Even though it was August, the air felt different, bracing and chilly compared to the stifling humidity we'd experienced in Mexico.

Martina rolled down her window and leaned out into the night, shouting, "It's *muy frio*! It's so, so cold!" And then, a few minutes later, she started screaming, "*Te amo*, Miguel! I love you!"

I tipped my head back and laughed, the happiest man on earth because Martina was finally by my side.

■ ■ ■

Not long after my wedding, Steve Buholzer asked for my help. "I want to make queso fresco," he said, "and sell it to some of the markets that serve Mexican immigrants, but the cheese never hardens the right way. Can you help us with the recipe, Miguel?"

"Sure," I said.

Queso fresco is a white, mild, crumbly cheese traditionally made from raw cow's milk. When Steve went through the recipe with me step by step, it was immediately obvious that they weren't using enough powdered milk. "The more powdered milk, the harder the body of the *queso* will be," I told him. "Let's adjust that in the recipe."

We started making the queso fresco in small batches. We made it at an extremely hot temperature, heating the milk and powder to 192 degrees and adding vinegar to lower the pH. The reason we did it this way is because a contaminated batch of fresh cheese from Jalisco Mexican Products Inc. had recently killed 62 people, leading the owners of the plant to close the plant and markets to strip their shelves of Jalisco cheeses.

The deaths were due to the cheese being contaminated with a bacteria that caused Listeria symptoms; obviously, at least some of the milk must not have been pasteurized. Steve didn't want to risk any bacteria growing in our products. To make doubly sure our queso fresco was safe, we pressed the cheese into tubes and put it into the cooler right away, then cut it up and wrapped it the next day.

The Klondike sales representatives hit the road in their trucks and took some samples of queso fresco to Texas. Not long after that, Steve called me into his office again.

"Oh, shit, I must be in trouble," I told Webster as I hurried into the office, but I was met by a grinning Steve.

"There's a guy on the phone, and I need you to talk to him for me, Miguel," Steve said. "He doesn't speak any English, but he wants to buy some of our queso fresco. Apparently, it's a huge hit in Texas."

I was nearly trembling with excitement. "Okay. What price should we put on it?"

"How about $1.60 a pound?" Steve suggested.

I shook my head and got on the phone, where I told the caller that the cost for this "special, Hispanic-style cheese" would be $3.60 a pound. The guy and I haggled some, but he quickly agreed. What's more, he wanted 6,000 pounds of it!

When I hung up and told Steve what I'd done, he gave me the thumb's up. I'd proven my worth as a cheesemaker.

■ ■ ■

I should have anticipated that, just as I had been homesick in the United States because I didn't speak English or understand the customs, Martina would be too. It was even worse for her because she had nothing to do all day but sit in the apartment. Even if she got up at 3 a.m. to drive me to work so she could keep the car, she had nobody to visit and nowhere to go. This was a far cry from Martina's exciting life at the university with her friends. It was even worse than being at home with her parents. At least in Irapuato, Martina had her sisters and friends, and didn't have to struggle to understand what was on television.

While for me everything was better with Martina here, it became clear within a few weeks that she needed a job to fill her empty hours. With no English, few skills, no college degree, and no work visa, it was difficult for her to find employment. Eventually she found a job cutting up carpets for a factory, but it was brutal work, and she was ill-suited for it.

And then one day Martina came to me with news that made me almost as happy as our wedding day: "Miguel, I think I'm pregnant," she said.

We were still so young—I was 24 years old, and she was only 22—but this was the culmination of our dreams, the realization of everything we'd longed for since first falling in love as teenagers. Even back then, all those years ago, I knew I wanted to be a father; I suppose I craved family life because I'd never had a good one. Now, looking back after so many decades of experience, I marvel at my youthful certainty. How can you know when you fall in love that it will last forever?

The short answer is that you can't. All you can do is follow your heart, and that's what I was doing. Everything I did in my life, I did for love.

Martina was nauseated from the pregnancy and soon gave up her job cutting carpets, while I took extra shifts at Klondike to make more money. The Buholzer brothers and Webster were already fathers, so they were supportive and happy to help me find more work. This meant I was away from home even more, leaving Martina feeling isolated and depressed.

Two months after Martina discovered she was pregnant, we were at home together on a weekend when she went to the bathroom and returned in tears. Her face was chalk-white. "I'm bleeding, Miguel," she said. "I think I'm losing the *bebe*."

I jumped up from the sofa and called the first person I could think of who might know what to do: Steve's wife, Thea Buholzer. She was at our apartment within minutes and drove us straight to the hospital emergency room. There, the doctor did an ultrasound.

"It's an ectopic pregnancy," he said, and explained it was also called a "tubal pregnancy" because the fertilized egg had implanted in one of Martina's fallopian tubes. Our child never had a chance to grow.

I felt sick with sorrow, but my first concern was caring for Martina. All tubal pregnancies must end because a fetus can't grow outside the womb. Today, most can be terminated with the injection of a drug called methotrexate, but back then surgery to remove the egg was the only option. Martina would have to be admitted to the hospital for the procedure and stay there for two days. She would then be on bed rest for a week.

I had to work to support us, so I was happy when Martina called her mom and, after breaking down in tears, asked if she would come and help take care of her. I didn't want my wife to be alone during a time like this. Martina's mother agreed at once and arrived two days later, while Martina was recovering from the surgery. I picked up my mother-in-law at the airport and drove her straight to the hospital, relieved that Martina would have this extra family support.

I was completely blindslided a few days later, when I discovered that Martina's mom was still campaigning to break us up. Somehow, while she was sitting by Martina's bedside at the hospital, the topic of religion had come up.

"We should pray for you and the *bebe*," my mother-in-law had said. "Which church do you belong to here, *mi hija*?"

"We don't go to church *aqui*," Martina said.

Her mother was aghast. She had always prided herself on being a devout Catholic, just like my own mother. "No? But *porque*? Surely there must be a Catholic church not too far away."

"It's not that. It's because Miguel doesn't believe in God," Martina said. "I don't think I do, either."

"He doesn't believe?" her mother cried. "Then you must divorce Miguel at once! You can't stay married to *un hombre* who doesn't believe in *Dios*. We'll have the marriage annulled. You're young. You'll fall in love and marry again. Come home, where *Papi* and I can take care of you."

Martina repeated this conversation to me when I picked her up from the hospital. I was in shock. At home, I tucked Martina into bed, then went into the kitchen to confront my mother-in-law, yelling, "Who do you think you are, coming here and trying to tear us apart when we've just lost our *bebe*? What kind of person *does* that?"

Our argument raged on until I went to bed in disgust. That night, as I lay with Martina, she turned to me and said, "The thing is, Miguel, I don't want a divorce, but I *want* to go home. I need my *madre* to take care of me. And I don't want to live in Monroe anymore. I don't like it here. I'm sorry."

And, just like that, the fight died in me. Of course Martina was sad. She'd been depressed living here already, and losing the baby had sent her into an even darker place. How could I refuse her, when she was so clearly hurting?

"All right, *mi amor*," I said quietly. "If that's what you want, I'll buy a ticket so you can go home for a little while. Then, when you're stronger, you can come back to me."

She shook her head and sat up. Her complexion was still pale and her hair was lank and straight. "That's the thing, Miguel. I don't think I can ever come back here. I want to be in *México*."

65

Create Opportunity

And, just like that, the dream I'd worked so hard to achieve went up in smoke.

However, at the age of 25, I had already mastered some important lessons about business—and about myself. The first lesson was to choose my friends wisely. I'd gotten into trouble all through high school partly because I'd chosen to hang out with friends who thought school was less important than fast cars, fast girls, and drinking until the sun comes up.

Since coming to the United States, I'd also learned essential lessons about the importance of working hard and paying attention. Doing so put me in the position of not only taking advantage of opportunities that came my way, but of creating my own opportunities where others saw none. And even though I sometimes failed to achieve my goals, like when Webster and I made our own cheese and sold it, I was discovering a core of resilience within myself. This tenacity would see me through another tough transition as I brought my new cheese-making skills back to Mexico.

Part II

FROM CHEESE CUTTER TO FACTORY OWNER

Chapter 4

Learn to Pivot

Be Flexible, but Ruthless with Your Time and Energy.

I had already given a pasteurizer, a homogenizer, and a separator to Don Poncho and Poncho to install in La Blanquita as part of my investment in their company. I'd also bought enough shares to ensure that I'd have a foothold in their business when I decided to move back to Mexico. My return to Mexico was happening sooner than I'd anticipated, but at least I had a plan in place.

For the next two months, while Martina recuperated from the miscarriage at home with her family, I continued working at Klondike and saving money. I communicated regularly with Poncho to ensure that the machinery I'd bought for La Blanquita would be installed and ready to use by the time I arrived.

Truthfully, once I threw myself into action, I was excited about this new venture. Martina and I could be happy in Mexico, I decided, close to our friends and family, and I'd prove to everyone—especially my in-laws—that Martina's faith in me was not misplaced. As part of our agreement, Poncho had bought me a small car and would offer me a salary of 20,000 pesos per month—the equivalent of $940/monthly by today's exchange rate. Not a fortune, even then, but enough for Martina and me to buy a small house and live comfortably.

Things went sideways right from the beginning, however. My intent was to make cheese from real milk—something Don Poncho had never done in his life—just like I'd learned to do in Wisconsin.

I was betting that people in Mexico would love US-style Monterrey Jack cheese. However, it turns out that Poncho, for all of his university training, was a terrible engineer; none of the machines I'd sent him for pasteurizing and homogenizing the milk were installed correctly.

I worked on the machines until they were functioning properly. Once I'd gotten over that first hurdle, I tried using the same recipe for Monterrey Jack I'd been relying on for over two years at Klondike, but somehow every batch failed. It took a while to pinpoint exactly why. I knew the recipes by heart, and I was using the same amount of milk and rennet. With Don Vicente, I'd learned that rennet is composed of an enzyme called chymosin that causes milk to coagulate, separating milk into curds and whey. This is typically a straightforward process. Yet, somehow the rennet never caused the milk to form curds when I made the cheese at La Blanquita. What the hell was going on?

Poncho and his father were drinking so heavily by then that neither paid much attention to what was actually happening inside the factory. I was the one on the floor making the cheese, or in the laboratory, supervising quality control. After testing my ingredients and running through the recipe countless times to examine different variables, I concluded that the only thing that could possibly be off was the milk.

To test this hypothesis, I asked one of the drivers to bring me to the dairy farm that provided La Blanquita with milk. The milk was delivered in 50-pound barrels covered with plastic lids—nothing like the stainless steel containers in the United States that could be sterilized clean.

To my shock, the delivery men picked up the milk, then stopped at a wall just outside the dairy barn. We parked our truck and climbed on top of it to see over the wall. Below, there were other barrels filled with milk and covered with flies; the milk clearly had manure floating in it too. As I watched, the men poured half of the milk from the barrels into other containers; added water, whey, and a dash of yellow color to fill the barrels back up; then reloaded them on the truck.

In a flash I understood what was happening: they were diluting the milk with whey to double their profits! This made me furious. In Wisconsin, I had seen firsthand what pride the dairy farmers took in the quality of their cows' pure output. They would *never* add even a drop of water to their pure milk. And, because the milk in Wisconsin was top quality, Wisconsin cheese was among the best in the world. Now, these guys were selling me diluted milk and thinking I wouldn't notice!

I yanked my camera out and began photographing the crooks in action so I could prove what was going on to Don Poncho. Unfortunately, the delivery guys spotted me and came after me with a pistol.

"Give me the fucking camera, man," the gunman shouted, "and nobody gets hurt!"

I had no choice. I handed over the camera. The gunman smashed it beneath a boot heel, laughing.

To my shock, when I returned to La Blanquita and told Don Poncho what I'd discovered, he simply laughed. "I've been using those guys for years, and we make perfectly good *queso* without milk," he boasted.

"Well, I want to make cheese with top quality *leche*," I grumbled, and that was the last time I ever used those delivery guys.

■ ■ ■

As the months passed, I began feeling trapped. Yes, I was making improvements at the factory little by little—for instance, I decided that there had to be a better way to stretch that hot Oaxaca cheese and designed a Teflon-coated machine that could take over that

71

task—but the future didn't look promising. My title at La Blanquita was head of production, but how could I do my job successfully and grow the business, if Poncho and Don Poncho didn't take anything seriously except how much liquor they could consume every week?

La Blanquita was hemorrhaging money. Don Poncho was supposedly managing the administration and financial end of things, but he had used the money I invested in the company to build fancy new offices rather than put it back into better equipment and employee training. He had also taken out so many loans against the business that I had no idea how we'd ever dig ourselves out of the red.

Poncho, who allegedly headed up our sales efforts, was always scheming, trying to get rich quick without doing any actual hard work. His latest gamble was Amway, a pyramid scheme of selling soap and other household products door to door; he spent many more hours doing that than selling cheese.

Unfortunately, I had sunk too much of my savings into La Blanquita for me to leave, and now Martina was expecting our first child. We were thrilled by the prospect of becoming parents, but I lay sleepless and terrified next to my wife at night, wondering if Don Poncho's factory would go under and suck me down with it.

Days were better because I could work hard enough to push my anxiety aside and focus on producing quality cheese. I devoted countless hours in the factory's lab to testing different processes and tweaking recipes. Poncho wanted me to make cheese with a longer shelf life, so we could start selling to the big-box chain stores farther away, instead of limiting our business only to the small mom-and-pop markets around town. Naturally I was keen to do that as well, to increase our profit margin, but how?

One day, I hit on an amazingly simple idea: What if we froze the cheese as soon as we made it? That could keep it safe by prohibiting the mold to grow on it while extending the shelf life. Was that even possible?

To find out, I drove to Salamanca, to a laboratory known for its food processing and preservation methods, and asked the secretary if they had any food engineers I could speak to about an idea.

"What kind of idea?" She eyed me suspiciously.

"Just a small thought about how to extend the shelf life of *queso*," I said.

"Wait here," she said with a sniff, and disappeared through a door.

Just as I was wondering whether I'd hit another road block, a man appeared, wearing a white lab coat and glasses. "Hector Obregon," he introduced himself and offered me his hand to shake.

I gave him my name and explained my theory. Later, Hector would tell me that the secretary had come to him and said, "Some crazy guy is in the office and you need to get rid of him fast," but he listened to me with interest that day. Then he rubbed his chin and gazed at me thoughtfully. "So let me get this straight. You want to freeze the cheese you make, so it will last longer in the truck on its way to stores?"

"*Exactamente*. Is that possible? It would have to be a quick process," I added. "Otherwise, the *queso* might grow bacteria."

"We'd have to flash freeze it," he mused, "maybe in liquid carbon dioxide. Can you bring me some of your product?" He seemed excited now, bouncing on his toes like a kid waiting to open a birthday present.

Over the next few weeks, I brought Hector samples of our cheese. He also drove out to La Blanquita to observe our operation, make notes, and conduct experiments. His company eventually invested in the idea of freezing cheese and made it work; ultimately, Hector won an innovation award for our new process.

The procedure for freezing cheese was beautifully practical. We installed a metal tunnel at La Blanquita, something that looked like a big clothes dryer, but worked in the opposite way. Instead of heating objects up to dry them, we hooked up a gas line that emitted carbon dioxide to flash-freeze the cheese as it moved through the tunnel on a conveyor belt. The frozen cheese was shrink-wrapped in plastic immediately, so nothing could contaminate it before it was packaged and loaded onto transport trucks. Everyone was delighted with the outcome, and our profit margin grew as we expanded our market reach.

Meanwhile, I also continued pushing for cleaner, more efficient production facilities at La Blanquita. "I'm sick and tired of working in a place that stinks like a sewer!" I yelled at Don Poncho one day in exasperation. "We have to clean this equipment more often and teach the workers to sanitize the machines."

But the more I argued on behalf of investing in the equipment and workers we needed to make higher quality cheese, the more hours Don Poncho spent in his office getting drunk or out spending money on inconsequential luxuries. Poncho was nearly always absent from work, so I was fighting an uphill battle alone to improve the factory. I could see the writing on the wall: the factory was going to have to shut down in the near future. Desperately, I searched for other career paths, even selling cattle food for my cousin Alejandro on the side, hoping that opportunity might lead me somewhere if I couldn't turn things around at La Blanquita.

"Miguel, they're going to fire you from La Blanquita if you keep arguing with them," my brother Pedro, who was married to Don Poncho's daughter, confided in me one day. "You've got to learn to keep your *boca* shut."

"How can I do that, when Don Poncho and Poncho are preventing me from making any progress with the company?" I demanded.

Our latest battle had been about a cheese factory Poncho sent me to see in Lagos de Moreno. The factory was next to a river thick with sewage, yet Poncho wanted me to buy cheese from them that we could distribute to our retailers. I refused and told him we should make the cheese ourselves because we could do it cheaper and better.

By then, Martina had given birth to our first child, Cristobal. Having a son transformed me completely. I wept as I stared down at that tiny, red, wrinkled newborn face and vowed to redouble my efforts to build a stable future for my family. I never wanted my son to suffer or want for anything. Unlike my own childhood, I wanted his to be safe and financially secure, and rich in love. But it seemed impossible to do that at La Blanquita. I'd have to find another path.

Then one day a stranger came to La Blanquita, and my fate changed yet again.

■ ■ ■

It was the middle of the morning at the factory. When I emerged from the lab, I discovered that Don Poncho had company. The stranger was heavyset and dark skinned with a pencil-thin mustache. He broke out in a grin when he saw me.

"Holy shit, *los Americanos* are here!" he said, noting my American-made boots and blue eyes.

The man's name was Juan. Originally from Lagos de Moreno, one of the largest cities in the state of Jalisco, he and his brothers owned a company based in California that provided cheese and other products to retail stores and restaurants that catered largely to Latinx immigrants in the United States.

Don Poncho asked me to show Juan around Guanajuato and introduce him to some of the other cheese factory owners. One of the factories was located in Queretero, a place known for its strip clubs. Juan insisted on stopping at one. I had a couple of drinks while he disappeared into the back room with not just one, but two of the table dancers. When he emerged, laughing and invigorated, I drove him back to La Blanquita, trying not to look at his gold wedding ring.

That afternoon, Juan invited Don Poncho out for a meal and suggested that I join them. I accepted the invitation, surprised to be included. Don Poncho rarely treated me like an equal despite my hard work and financial investment in the company.

At the restaurant, when Don Poncho excused himself to go to the restroom, Juan hurriedly handed me his business card. "Listen, the real reason I came to Mexico is because I need to recruit someone to join our company and teach my guys how to make Mexican cheese," he said. "You'd be perfect for the job. What do you think, Miguel? Want to come work for me in California?"

"Maybe," I said.

I was startled by the offer, and uncomfortable with the idea of going behind Don Poncho's back. He'd given me my first real job after high school and trusted me to run his factory's day-to-day production. Besides, what would Martina think of this idea? She was happy in Mexico. Our son, Cristobal, was only a year old, and it was wonderful having family and friends around. Would she be willing to return to the United States?

I was also wary of Juan's easy charm. Could I trust him, or would I face the same bullshit working for him that I faced here with Don Poncho and his son? I was tired, plain and simple, of being surrounded by idiots whose work ethic didn't match my own.

On the other hand, La Blanquita's finances were such a disaster that Don Poncho would likely have to declare bankruptcy soon. They had me by the balls because of the money I'd invested, but I knew Pedro was probably right, and they were looking for a reason to fire me. Maybe it would be smart to jump out of the boat before it sank.

That night, I went home to Martina and explained the situation. "I know you're happy living here, *mi amor*, but the truth is that I don't see any future for us with Don Poncho and La Blanquita," I said.

She nodded. "You need to at least go to California and check it out," she said. "If you see the factory for yourself and spend more time with this Juan guy, you'll know what to do. I'll support you a hundred percent no matter what you decide."

I kissed her, relieved to have Martina's blessing, and went to call Juan with my decision.

■ ■ ■

Juan's company was located outside of San Jose, California. I was shocked by the size of the company; they produced and sold not only cheese products, but other Mexican comestibles, like packaged chorizo and jarred sauces. The sales were probably over a billion a year.

Fortunately, I'd managed to save my green card from being thrown into the trash while Martina was cleaning, so I was able to enter the United States legally. This was a relief. I'd been lucky when it came to getting that green card. About a month after working for Klondike under the false Social Security number Jorge Moreno had given me, Thea had called me into the office and said, "Miguel, I'm sorry, but you have to fix this. We can't have people working for Klondike illegally. Listen, there's a new amnesty program for immigrant farm workers. Maybe you can get a green card that way."

Terrified of losing my job at Klondike, I had driven straight to a church in Rockford, Illinois, where people were helping immigrants with paperwork. A woman there had counseled me and given me the necessary papers. Because I had been helping the dairy farmers unload their milk at Klondike and had made friends with several of them, they were happy to sign the papers to support my amnesty claim. I took the papers back to the church, and in 1988, I was given a green card allowing me to work legally under that US amnesty program. Now, since I still had that card, I could travel legally to California and work for Juan, who promised to sponsor me for American citizenship if I stayed with his company.

I took some vacation days from La Blanquita and flew to California by myself. It was immediately clear that Juan's factory, while busier and cleaner than La Blanquita, wasn't set up well. They had expanded the original building as they increased their production, but they'd added rooms in a slipshod way, without any visible plan to streamline their operations. As Juan showed me around, my brain buzzed with excitement. He made it clear I'd have free rein to make changes in the production process. He also promised to give me a decent operating budget, in addition to a generous salary of $80,000 a year, plus moving expenses and $20,000 for each new cheese recipe.

When I returned to Mexico, I explained the situation to Martina. "This is a great opportunity for our family. He has a solid business," I told her. "We'd have plenty of money and I'd have a challenging position. But I'm only going to do it if you're willing to come with me to California."

"I am," Martina said, and so it was settled.

I gave my notice to a very displeased Don Poncho and arrived in California a month later to oversee cheese production at my new company. Juan was hoping I'd show his team of employees—nearly all Mexican immigrants—how to make queso fresco, panela, Oaxaca cheese, cotija cheese, and crema. Although the workers were Mexican—a very different environment from the one at Klondike—I kept to myself and didn't socialize with them, preferring to concentrate on my job. I had burned my bridges at La Blanquita; I couldn't afford to fail at this new opportunity.

Martina, Cristobal, and I stayed at Juan's house for the first two months. Juan's wife, Pamela, was lovely and welcoming, a short-haired, wide-hipped woman who was a wonderful mother to their two children. Getting to know Pamela made me increasingly uncomfortable with Juan's rampant infidelities. He'd bought a new, champagne-colored Mercedes, one of the luxury models, and constantly used it to pick up girls and bring them to the factory, where they'd drink and have sex in his office.

"Come on, Miguel, let's have a *poquito* fun," he'd say. "Join us!"

The House that Cheese Built

Sometimes he'd take the girls out for a meal or to a bar, and occasionally he pestered me enough that I joined him, but I never cheated on Martina. I would be lying if I said I wasn't tempted occasionally, but I confided in Martina about what was going on. If I couldn't be truthful with her, I knew I'd feel suffocated. Of course Martina hated what Juan was doing to Pamela. The two women were together with the children all day and had become friends.

Juan was already rich and felt entitled to do whatever pleased him. He employed other people like me to do the actual work of making cheese and managing the factory operations so he could play. I didn't have that luxury. I had no parents to support me, La Blanquita was going under, and I had no plan B.

I pretended to laugh along with his antics, but in reality Juan's easy attitude toward infidelity chilled me to the bone. I couldn't help but think of all of the times my mother had suffered because of my father's womanizing.

One childhood memory was particularly haunting. I was probably about 13 years old when my father invited me to accompany him on a trip to Guadalajara, where he had "some pressing business to attend to," he told my mother. I was excited to ride into the city and flattered that my father had asked me to accompany him, since he typically barely even acknowledged my existence. Only later did it occur to me that my mother must have insisted he take me on this journey. She probably hoped my presence would deter him from seeking out other women.

It didn't. My father drove us to see his friend, Nieto, in Guadalajara. Nieto and his wife owned a dance school in the city and lived in the house behind it. Several of the dancers hung around after classes as my father and Nieto got the grill going and began cooking. My father had started drinking, of course, and when he caught me watching him flirt with the girls, he narrowed his eyes.

79

Learn to Pivot

"Get me a drink, kid, and keep your mouth shut," he had snarled. "Don't tell your mother anything about this. What she doesn't know can't hurt her."

I had obeyed and brought him a coke and rum. After that, I hung around in the doorway, still watching him with the girls—at this point, he had his arms around one of them and was kissing her—until my father suddenly advanced toward me, shouting, "Get the fuck out of here!"

He'd morphed into The Transformer again. I hated myself for still being scared of him—I was nearly as tall as he was by then—but I truly was afraid, so I ran upstairs, angry and close to tears.

We spent the night at Nieto's house, where I slept in the bedroom with their son and my father closed himself in one of the other bedrooms with the dancer. The next day, I told him it was time to leave, but he refused to come home with me.

Instead, my father had driven me to the bus station, where he dropped me off with no money. I had enough change in my pocket to buy a bus ticket to Guanajuato, but no food. I must have looked as hungry and miserable as I felt, because a nice guy offered to buy my breakfast. When we arrived at the station, I walked several miles to my house. I had planned to lie to my mother about why I was arriving alone, not because I was loyal in any way to my father, but because I didn't want to hurt her. She took one look at me, however, and knew I was upset.

"What is it? What happened?" she asked. "Where's your father?"

She kept asking questions, until finally I broke down and told her the truth. She wasn't surprised by my father's behavior; she was simply exhausted. My brothers and I again tried to convince her to divorce him after this incident, but of course she refused to even consider the idea. My mother still went to Mass every Sunday and dedicated her life to God. As she saw the world, God's will provided an immutable blueprint for her life, and good Catholics did not divorce their spouses.

Growing up and witnessing my parents' disastrous marriage had made me even less inclined to believe in God. What's more, it made me determined to honor and cherish my own marriage, and my wife, by being faithful to Martina. Every time Juan tried to distract me with women and drink, I focused even harder at work.

There was a lot to focus on. My first task was to streamline the production process so we could make different cheeses and a greater volume of products. It soon became clear that this would be tough to do at the current facility. Juan was a high-energy, nervous guy, especially around the brothers he partnered with; they were in charge of the company's other food products and left it up to Juan to manage the cheese factory. When I told Juan he needed to buy a new factory because the current facility was at full capacity, he asked if I'd come to a meeting with his brothers and present the case for doing this. I was surprised but willing to try.

The meeting went well. I explained the need for expanding into a different facility in blunt terms, saying, "You can't produce enough inventory in your current factory. You need to start looking for another one, *pronto*."

Juan and his brothers had started their company in 1981, just two years before I arrived, as a small business built around selling homemade artisanal Mexican cheeses and creams to local stores. They wanted to expand that business to compete in the global marketplace, so they agreed with my suggestion to move the operation to a new location. The solution presented itself in Hanford, California, where Safeway was selling an enormous plant where they'd been making cottage cheese. With my input, the Marquez family bought the plant, ditched some of Safeway's old equipment, and installed new machines to make the production process more efficient, including a tunnel jacket for freezing the cheese we produced.

As we were doing this rehab work, we discovered a giant sink-hole beneath the factory floor, right where the milk vats were. We had to refill that area with cement, and it cost quite a bit. We also had to remove the asbestos to remain in compliance with OSHA regulations. Juan was pissed off about these extra expenditures, but I remained calm and told him to let me handle things.

"We can't skip steps just to save *dinero*," I reminded him. "If we do, we'll run into other, worse *problemas* down the line."

To set up the factory, I contacted Webster, my old friend from Klondike. He had connections with Darlington Dairy Supply. They were happy to sell us the equipment we needed and helped us set up our operations in California.

Because Hanford was nearly 90 miles from San Jose, and because I'd grown increasingly weary of lying to Juan's wife, Pamela, about her husband's adulterous behavior, Martina and I decided to move out of his family's home and into an apartment close to the new factory. It was a one-bedroom apartment, and we had no furniture other than a mattress on the floor, a couple of chairs, and a rickety table, but we didn't care about owning new things, preferring instead to keep saving money. Besides, the apartment complex was clean and had a pool, and now we could truly breathe in our own space and have some privacy as a family.

Despite the new apartment, I wasn't completely sold on living in California. People always complain about traffic in southern California, but the real drawback for me was that we were living in an earthquake zone. Once, Martina and I were at the zoo with Cristobal when there was a tremendous outcry from the animals: birds caw-ing, lions roaring, bears bellowing. Then the ground began shaking under our feet. I thought I'd faint from fright!

Another time, we were in the apartment with Cristobal when the light fixtures began trembling overhead and the table and chairs danced in the kitchen. Every time we experienced an earthquake,

I remembered the devastation in Mexico City after the earthquake that had killed my father. No way did I want to lose my family beneath a toppled building.

■ ■ ■

As the months flew by, I continued testing and improving recipes for Juan. He'd been trying to make queso fresco, for example, but it tasted and acted too much like panela. Panela is the Mexican version of cottage cheese in the United States; it's made from skimmed, pasteurized cow's milk and is creamy and mild to the taste, with a milky aroma. You can compare it to Indian paneer; when you heat it, panela cheese will soften without melting.

Queso fresco has some similar properties to panela, but needs to be drier and crumble better between your fingers. With Don Poncho, I'd used a homogenizer—a machine that forces the cheese through fine openings against a hard surface—to help break up the chemical chains and elasticity of the fresh cheese, so I decided to try hooking up the homogenizer to the pasteurizer line at Juan's factory. The results were even better than I'd hoped: the queso fresco now crumbled exactly as it did at home. Nobody was doing this yet in the United States, and Juan's sales of queso fresco skyrocketed as a result. He and his brothers were very excited by the result, and Juan paid me $20,000 for the new recipe. He kept the recipe a secret and took full credit for it from his brothers, but that was fine with me. It was his factory, and he'd hired me to do this.

Next, I put in a big metal tunnel to freeze the cheese with carbon dioxide before it was packaged, just as I'd done at Don Poncho's. This allowed us to package the queso fresco without anyone's hands touching it and potentially contaminating the product. They had already been using a machine in Juan's factory to package the cheese, but I added conveyor belts so the cheese would be frozen and packaged three times faster with no risk of bacterial cultures.

The cotija recipe took a little more trial and error. I'd made cotija with raw milk for Don Vicente. In the United States, the milk was pasteurized, which meant the flavor of the milk was altered. However, I remembered how, at Klondike, we had added goat's lysase to the cow's milk to give it a sharper taste, one that was similar to cotija cheese. I played around in Juan's lab with this recipe until I'd found the perfect ingredients for a sharp cotija flavor.

For each new recipe, Juan kept his promise and paid me another $20,000. Because I was still distrustful of the business, I put every penny of that $40,000 windfall, along with most of my salary, into the bank. However, when Martina's father and uncle decided to divide the dairy farm and Martina's father was left without any cows, I immediately offered to help.

I used my savings to buy 150 cows for my father-in-law, as well as a milking machine, and shipped them from Wisconsin to his farm. I never expected him to repay me. That's what family was for, and by now Martina's family was my own.

■ ■ ■

Juan was pleased with my work and told me so, but his focus on the factory continued to be diluted by his love of women. On one trip, for instance, we traveled to Tijuana together. We'd asked an engineer in Michoacán to make a special grinder for the factory. When we needed to meet the FDA (Food and Drug Administration) inspector at the border to have the machine examined so we could get permission to install this particular machine part in the factory, Juan invited me to come along.

Naturally, when we arrived in Tijuana, the city just across the border from San Diego, California, Juan was eager to show me the sights. And by that, I mean he was eager to show me one particular street crowded with brothels and prostitutes calling out things like, "I can give you a blow job *for veinte dollares*, or a hand job *por diez*." Every sort of pleasure was on sale at bargain basement rates. I felt like I'd landed in hell and desperately wanted to retreat to my hotel room.

Juan had other ideas. "Come on, Miguel. Live a little!" he begged. "Martina never needs to know. We're not even in the same country as our *esposas*!" he added drunkenly, as he careened down the street with a woman on each arm and others following behind. The more women, the merrier, as far as Juan was concerned. He obviously felt like a king here.

"No, *gracias*," I said, for his words were an echo of my father's at that dance school, so long ago. I couldn't even imagine touching these poor prostitutes, many of whom were only young girls, never mind having sex with them.

We spent just one night in Tijuana, but even that was one night too many. Early the next morning, Juan appeared at the door of my hotel room, rumpled and sleepy and very happy. On the drive back to San Jose, he told me stories about having sex not only with women, but with goats too! After that, I could hardly look him in the eye. I certainly didn't want to shake his hand.

When I told Martina about this incident, she flew off the handle. "Pamela can't stay with that *idiota*!" she declared. "What if he gives her a disease?"

"It's not our business," I reminded her. "*Por favor* don't say anything to her. It could cost me my job. Besides, I'm guessing Pamela knows what he's like and looks the other way because Juan provides well for her and the children."

I thought the matter was settled between us. A few days later, however, Juan called me into his office, furious because Pamela had received a letter saying he was cheating on her. What's more, the letter had been written in the company's San Jose office. Pamela knew this because the typewriter in that office had one key that was slightly bent, so it hit the paper above the other letters.

Learn to Pivot

"Who sent my wife this *pinche* letter?" Juan demanded. "Was it Martina? She's the only one who would do this, and she has access to my office!" He waved the envelope at me. "Look at this postmark. It's definitely from your wife!"

I was terrified. I'd never seen Juan so angry. I couldn't afford to lose this job. Besides, I loved my job. "Let me *hablar con* Martina," I said. "I'll get to the bottom of this."

I went home that night and lit into Martina, who immediately confessed that she'd sent the letter. "And I'm not sorry, either!" Martina yelled. "Juan's a cheating, lying piece of *caca*, and Pamela should leave him!"

"Maybe so, but *no es* our business!" I shouted back, scaring even myself as well as Martina, because I rarely let myself get angry. I was always afraid that lurking somewhere deep within me lay a Transformer with my father's cruel temper. "We need to figure out a way to fix *esto*, or I might get fired. Is that what you want? Huh? Is it?"

"Of course not," Martina said, pouting now.

Eventually, we decided that the best way to fix the situation was to have Martina write another letter on the same typewriter, then send it from San Jose. Since we were living in Hanford by then, Pamela would be confused; she'd suspect someone else who lived in San Jose must be sending her these inflammatory letters.

In the end, Pamela couldn't know for sure if the letter writer was Martina, and even though I confessed the truth to Juan, he forgave me. "Just promise me she'll never do that again," he said.

I did. "Just *por favor*, please stop asking me to join you when you're with other women, so I can focus on work," I begged. He agreed.

"Remember that we can't dictate how other people live, only ourselves," I told Martina that night. "What's important isn't what Juan and Pamela do in their marriage, but how you and I behave in our

The House that Cheese Built

own. I promise that I will never, ever cheat on you, no matter how much Juan tries to tempt me."

Of course, I should have asked Martina to promise the same thing, but it never occurred to me. I was too busy creating recipes that would one day become the cornerstone of my own cheese-making business.

Here's the thing about success: sometimes you can't know how successful you're going to be, and you don't recognize the sacrifices you're making along the way. Yes, I had learned to pivot, first by making cheese in Mexico under extremely difficult circumstances, and then by returning back to the United States, where I was able to continue perfecting my recipes and learning how to manage production on a large scale. My passion for mastering the business drove me forward, and I was grateful for my relentless drive toward success. I was providing a good living for my family and proving everyone who'd ever doubted me wrong.

But at what cost to my personal health and marriage?

To all of you entrepreneurs out there, I urge you to continue creating opportunities and being ruthless with your time and energy as you follow your passion and tenacity forward. However, there are points where it's equally important to slow down and step back to evaluate what truly matters.

Chapter 5

Doing Business with the Amish

Adopt a Mindset of Making It Happen No Matter What.

About a year into my time with Juan's company, he arranged for me to apply for US citizenship. The written test was going to be difficult for me, since I had trouble reading and writing in Spanish, and this test would be in English. Martina helped me study the US Constitution so that I could answer questions about it as well as questions about American history and government.

That was hard enough, but the section of the test that really scared me was the face-to-face interview where I'd have to answer questions and write something in English on the spot. Fortunately, I had a great tutor: Martina wrote "The sky is blue" in English for me to copy over and over, and I sailed through the interview and writing sample.

The swearing-in ceremony was held in an auditorium. I stood with a hundred other immigrants to plead allegiance to the United States. The only hitch that day was confusion over my birthday. On my Mexican birth certificate, my birthday is July 12, 1964, the day my drunk father gave the clerk, but my mom told me I was actually born on July 6. When I received my citizenship papers, I saw that they'd listed my birthday as July 14, 1964.

I decided to just leave it and give myself three birthday parties a year. Becoming a US citizen was nothing I'd ever planned to do in my life, but the night I was sworn in, I felt both an overwhelming relief—in the back of my mind, I'd always worried about being deported, even with a green card—and an immense sense of gratitude. Working in the United States had taught me so much about hard work, and it was good to live in a country where hard work really does pay off.

■ ■ ■

As Webster and I continued setting up the new factory for Juan, another opportunity knocked. This time it was Webster who proposed a change: "What would you think about going into business with me, Miguel?"

"You mean, independently?" I asked in *sorpresa*. "Just the two of us?"

"Yes." Webster told me about a cheese-making contest being run by an Amish community in Ohio. "They're looking for master cheese-makers," he said. "If we win the contest, they'll build us a factory and supply us with the milk."

I was immediately suspicious. "How do you win the contest?"

"Simple. You make the best cheddar *queso* they've ever tasted," he said.

I grinned. "Well, we certainly know how to do that."

I didn't expect to win the contest, truthfully, but I was keen to try. I knew that running our own cheese factory operation would be endless hours of work. I was supervising 150 employees for Juan, and I understood exactly how much labor was involved in producing quality products. I started early, usually around five o'clock in the morning, and never made it home until after seven o'clock. I worked weekends, too, which meant I rarely had time with Martina and Cristobal, who were often asleep when I left and back in bed again by the time I came home. Some nights I even slept in the factory to make sure everything was going right.

But if Webster and I were on our own, all of those hours would really mean something: we'd be creating a business we could call our own, with the profit going directly to us. I would also be happy to get out of California and move back to the Midwest. I imagined Martina would be glad to have me work with someone honorable, like Webster, too, instead of with Juan, who continued indulging himself with hookers and binge drinking.

When the time came for Webster and me to compete, I flew to Wisconsin, where Webster introduced me to the Amish representatives. I helped him make a 40-pound block of cheddar cheese, then flew home and tried to put the contest out of my mind, knowing we were competing with five other cheesemakers.

A month later, Webster called. "We won, Miguel, we won!" he crowed. I'd never heard my friend sound this excited. "We did it! We're finally going to have our own factory!"

I hung up the phone, my mouth dry with a combination of fear and excitement. This was it, the opportunity Webster and I had both been working toward. Now we'd be partners, and the success or failure of our business would all be on us.

Martina was in the living room watching TV. I sat down beside her and stared straight ahead like a zombie, swallowed by a sudden sinkhole of anxiety. Was I risking too much? What if I failed? I never wanted my family to suffer poverty the way mine had as a child. With Juan, at least I could count on having a secure job and a steady paycheck. What if I threw that all away for nothing?

On the other hand, you can dream up the very best ideas in the world, but if you don't test them out, how can you prove they're worth anything? Nothing will ever happen if you just sit in a corner and watch other people. If I didn't try my utmost to achieve my goal of being in business for myself, I'd always be a lost dreamer like my father.

The next time Martina turned to look at me on the couch, I swallowed hard and said, "Honey, *yo tengo* something to tell you."

■ ■ ■

Webster and I would be working around the clock to start our factory from the ground up with the Amish community in Middlefield, Ohio, so Martina and I decided it would be best for her to take Cristobal to Mexico and stay with her family for a few months. Meanwhile, I moved into an apartment with Webster and our old friend Kevin Weiss from Klondike, who had offered to help us get this new venture off the ground. Webster and Kevin were both married, but they hadn't brought their wives, either, so the three of us threw all of our energy into working, survived on cheap takeout food, and collapsed onto our inflatable mattresses at night.

I knew little about the Amish community before moving to Ohio. Over time, I learned that they were Protestants who were originally Mennonites, but broke off from that group because of theological differences. After first migrating from Europe to Pennsylvania in the 1700s, the Amish arrived in Ohio in the early 1800s. By the early 1990s, about 90,000 Amish people were living in North America. Most still sustained themselves through agriculture.

The reason the Amish needed Webster and me to run their factory was because living their version of a "Godly lifestyle" meant refusing to use any modern-day conveniences. They milked cows by hand, delivered the milk by horse and buggy, and needed Webster and me to help them build and run an efficient, mechanized cheese factory and make deals on the phone. We would buy milk from their farms for 50 cents a pound and make cheddar cheese they could sell to Kraft and in their markets.

At one point, I stopped by Nevin's house—he was the Amish man in charge of the factory after we won the contest—and I was fascinated to see that his house had no mirrors and none of the Amish had buttons on their clothing. The women were covered head-to-toe in long skirts, caps, and aprons, and their faces were devoid of makeup.

We were different, true, but I admired our Amish partners because they were generous and hard working. A group of Amish men built our factory by hand without using any power tools, and they did it in record time. I had started purchasing equipment with Webster to set things up, and by the time we received it two months later—mostly from Darlington Dairy Supply—the factory was already finished.

There were a few obstacles as we began producing cheese those first weeks. For instance, soon after we were underway, the pasteurizer started wheezing and making strange groaning noises, then conked out completely.

"What the hell happened?" I asked the men working for us.

Nobody knew. I tried closing off the valve to the milk silo, and when it wouldn't close, I opened the lid of the silo to figure out why. The Amish brought the milk to us in open cans and dumped it into troughs that were pumped into the silo. It turned out that some of the milk must have been contaminated by flies because it was open to the air; now maggots were passing through the valve, because one of the silos had a crack in it and was leaking milk between the silo's jacket and outside wall. We had to dump 100,000 pounds of milk so we could repair the whole system. After that, we built a second silo to make sure we could keep the factory running if that ever happened again.

■ ■ ■

Martina joined me in Ohio with Cristobal about a month after we opened the factory. For a while she lived in the apartment with Webster, Kevin, and me. It was a huge relief to have her cook and keep house for us, since we were working such long hours, but it didn't take Martina long to tire of this routine.

93

Doing Business with the Amish

"Miguel, we need our own place," she said. "I'm about to keel over with exhaustion."

I couldn't stand seeing Martina unhappy, so I agreed immediately. Because we were putting every cent we had into the factory, the only place I could afford to rent in Ohio was an apartment in a rundown complex. Martina didn't like it much. She was lonely there, since we were the only Mexicans around—the apartments were occupied by probably 60% Black residents and 40% White—and it was filthy besides. The walls were slimy to the touch, and the hallways stank of urine; the swimming pool steps were green with mold. The only good thing about the place was that Cristobal could pedal his tricycle in the parking lot.

We picked up stakes and moved once again a few months later, this time to a trailer in a mobile home park called Troy Oaks. It's a lucky thing we did, too: not long after we left the apartment building, the roof collapsed because nobody cleaned off the snow, and it was rotten.

■ ■ ■

The Amish had cosigned on a loan so Webster and I could buy equipment for the factory. At the start, we employed a dozen people—mostly Amish and all men, because the Amish women were relegated to selling cheese in their store. There still wasn't much of an immigrant community here, so our employees were locals, many of whom from families that had lived in the area for generations.

Webster and I handled every aspect of production. Though the Amish weren't allowed to operate any appliance with electricity in their homes, they could work on our machines through some magic loophole. Our contract stipulated that Webster and I would buy milk from the Amish at 50 cents a pound. They provided us with 150,000 pounds of milk every month, and I couldn't imagine how we'd ever use it all.

"Man, Webster, this is the real McCoy," I said, feeling panicked. "We have to prove we can do it right."

Taking a leap forward in your business can be a scary endeavor. All of us suffer from impostor syndrome to some degree; as our business grows, we wonder if we can tame the beast we've created.

However, as with with Don Poncho, I knew in my bones that working with Juan would curb my dreams. Staying with his company would doom me to never being anything greater than somebody's employee. I desired a bigger future, one where I could invest my time, energy, and focus into creating a product of my own and potentially reap bigger rewards. If you feel your passion calling to make something, and have the knowledge, experience, and energy to pursue it, you owe it to yourself to push past your fear of failure or you'll always regret it.

Chapter 6

Say Cheese

Push for Being Better at What You Do Every Day—Even 1% Better.

Webster and I were both hard workers and skilled cheesemakers. We had no trouble making high-quality cheddar cheese and Monterrey Jack from the milk the Amish farmers delivered. However, it quickly became apparent that the Amish were delivering far more milk than we required for the amount of cheese they were selling. What could we do with all of that extra milk?

After some thought, I became certain we could successfully tap into the market for Hispanic-style cheeses based on the growing number of immigrants I'd seen in Wisconsin and Illinois.

"What if we tried making Hispanic cheeses again?" I asked Webster.

"What kind?" he asked, scratching his head. "The Amish are giving us raw milk, and the quality isn't as high as what we were getting from the farmers who supplied Klondike."

This was true. The Amish milked by hand; if they touched the udder or any other part of the cow that came into contact with the milk, they transferred bacteria from themselves or from cow manure. With no refrigeration, they resorted to cooling their milk cans in streams, and the cans often didn't have lids. This meant the milk could also be contaminated by bird feces, insects, or even frogs. Oh yes. We'd seen it all.

That meant there was only one possibility. "We should make cotija *queso*," I said.

"What the hell is that?" Webster asked.

I explained, as best I could, what cotija was and what it should taste like, and how I'd perfected a cotija cheese recipe based on what I'd learned by working for Don Vicente and Juan. "If I succeed, I'd be the only Mexican making Mexican queso—all of the others in the Midwest are Americans," I added. "But the first thing we need to buy is a homogenizer."

"What for?" Webster frowned. "It's not like we're selling milk."

"No, but there are some cheese recipes, like the one for cotija, where, as soon as you put pressure on the *leche*, the cheese doesn't melt anymore because it breaks up the chemical chains. That's what people want in cotija: it's a dry cheese."

"This still doesn't make sense to me," he said.

"Do you trust me?"

"You know I do, Miguel."

We installed the homogenizer a few weeks later, and I made a test batch of cotija for Webster to taste. His eyebrows shot up in surprise. "That's pretty good stuff, Miguel."

I laughed. "Good. We're in business, then. All we need is a distributor."

■ ■ ■

Once we'd produced enough wheels of cotija to fill our rusty blue van, I set off for Chicago with Martina and Cristobal to keep me company. I knew this would be the closest Hispanic market near the Wisconsin border. "If I succeed at this, Martina, *tu* and *yo* will be in business for real," I said.

My wife was pregnant again; she shifted her bulk in the seat and smiled. "I have faith in you."

We drove slowly through a Hispanic neighborhood outside of downtown Chicago, stopping at small Mexican markets so I could go in and ask who was supplying them with cheese. My goal was to find the biggest distributor of Hispanic goods in the area. Various shopkeepers wanted to buy my cotija when they found out I was selling it, excited to find it was locally made. I asked each of them how much they'd be willing to pay, testing the market, so I'd have a better idea what to charge.

One vendor told me he could easily sell my cotija cheese for $8 per pound. "You and me, we'll split it 50/50," he offered.

I was tempted—this was a much higher price than I'd anticipated—but I declined. I only wanted to deal with one distributor.

Eventually, I found the man who was supplying most of the smaller stores and restaurants with Hispanic food products: Adolfo Vega at La Hacienda Brands. I parked in front of La Hacienda and slapped the van's dashboard, declaring, "This is it. I'm going to sell our *queso*!" to Martina before I went into the store.

I still hadn't decided on the final price for a wheel of cotija cheese, but I'd studied the American cheese market for years. Cheddar was selling for between $1.40 and $2.40 per pound at the time, but what I had was rare. Maybe I could sell it for more. When Mr. Vega came out to meet me, I told him I had cotija cheese for sale and decided to aim high, based on what some of the smaller shopkeepers had offered me for it.

"The thing is, this is a special artisan cotija *queso*, made by Mexican hands," I said. "I need to get $4.50 per pound at the very least." That would end up netting me $250 for a 60-pound wheel of cotija and a huge profit margin, since the cheese only cost 60 cents a pound to make.

Mr. Vega was short, dark-haired, and squarely built. He gave me a stern look and said, "Let me taste it and we'll see."

I cut off a small sliver of cheese and watched nervously as he chewed. After a minute, his eyes lit up. "Ah, tastes like home," he said. "I'll take the lot."

"All of it? At $4.50 per *libra*?" I'm sure I sounded shocked; I hadn't expected him to agree so readily.

"*Claro*," he said breezily, waving a hand. "Bring me all you've got in your truck."

"I'll need to be paid today," I said. "In cash." The truth was that I didn't yet have a bank account.

"*No problema*."

I hurriedly unloaded the 20 wheels of cheese, and he paid me on the spot, leading me into an office where people were counting bills and coins. Everyone—all of the Hispanic owners who were buying goods from Mr. Vega—must have been paying him in cash. I'd never seen so much money in one place! Mr. Vega counted out $5,000 in enormous piles of bills and said, "If I sell this *lote*, you can bet I'll be ordering more cotija from you, Miguel."

"Nice doing business with you," I said, trying to play it cool. Back at the van, though, I flashed the fat wad of bills in my pocket to Martina, who whooped with joy. She and I grabbed each other and kissed excitedly. "This is it, *mi amor*!" I said. "If he likes *este* cotija, our lives could change!"

Martina and I decided to celebrate by spending the night in Chicago. We found a hotel, and as we were pushing Cristobal's stroller down a street near Soldier Field stadium, we began seeing throngs of people. Many were speaking Spanish or Portuguese and were waving national flags. It took me a minute to clock what was happening: I'd been so excited about selling our cheese to Mr. Vega that I'd completely forgotten that the United States was hosting the 1994 FIFA World Soccer Cup. Today there was a game in Chicago!

Martina realized it at the same time. We clasped our hands together and nearly ran with the baby stroller as we searched for a ticket window. Miraculously, tickets were still available. We bought two tickets and stepped inside the stadium, where people were already cheering. This was an amazing opportunity. We'd always wanted to see the World Soccer Cup, and now here we were, enjoying this once-in-a-lifetime opportunity, thanks to my cheese and Mr. Vega. We couldn't have asked for a better celebration.

When we finally made our way home the next day, we were greeted by another terrific surprise: Mr. Vega had called, saying he wanted to buy two more pallets of cotija cheese.

"Hey," I said when I called Webster. "Guess what? I think we're going to need a bigger truck."

■ ■ ■

Webster and I bought a refrigerated truck from Darlington Dairy Supply soon after that. The first time I drove it to Mr. Vega's, Webster loaded the truck for me. It could handle 11 pallets of cheese, but Webster decided we could fit more 60-pound wheels of cheese into the truck if we did away with the pallets. We filled the truck to the top, and I drove off, excited to deliver my first full truckload of cotija cheese to Mr. Vega.

Halfway down the highway at 70 miles an hour, I hit a small bump, and the front wheels of the truck flew up in the air. Terrified, I slowed to a crawl. What the hell was going on with this truck?

When I reached the highway weighing station, I pulled onto the scale and waited. The guy in the booth shook his head at me. "I don't know, man. I think our scale must be busted. It says you've got like 80,000 pounds of cheese in this rig." He waved me through.

I swallowed hard. When I finally reached Mr. Vega's outside of Chicago after a painstakingly cautious drive, I unloaded the cheese. That took forever, too, and my back and shoulder muscles were burning with fatigue by the time I finished.

Say Cheese

"What the fuck were you thinking, putting so much *queso* in the truck?" I shouted when I got Webster on the phone. "The truck was rearing like a *pinche* horse!"

I had to hold the phone away from my ear, Webster was laughing so hard.

Despite this early fiasco, I continued driving to Mr. Vega's with truckloads of cotija cheese once a week, then twice a week as sales increased. That first year, we grossed $250,000 in sales despite having only Mr. Vega as our customer. He began pestering me about making different kinds of Hispanic-style cheeses.

"You'd make a killing Miguel, you really would," Mr. Vega said. "Nobody understands Mexican *quesos* like you do."

The problem, of course, was that the Amish had no interest in expanding their milk production, and there was only so much cheese I could make with this amount of milk. But I continued pondering the possibilities, especially now that Martina and I had just become parents to a second child, a daughter whom we named after her and called "Tuti."

I was delighted to have a daughter. My family seemed complete, especially when Martina's parents came to Ohio for Tuti's baptism. Although we were living simply to save money, my in-laws recognized how hard we were working, and how in love Martina and I were, and treated me like a son. We celebrated Tuti's baptism with ribs in a barbecue restaurant, and as I glanced around at my in-laws, wife, and two small children, I already felt like a success. I had married the woman I'd loved at first sight. Now we had two children and a business of our own. What more could a man ask for? My heart was overflowing with joy.

With two children, I was more determined than ever not only to succeed in business, but to be the sort of parent my father never was: patient and loving. I only slipped up once when Cristobal was young, maybe four years old. Martina and I had taken the kids to

Chicago on one of my rare Sunday afternoons off, and we were pushing my daughter's stroller across the street toward Navy Pier when a cab careened toward us. The driver stopped at the intersection, but blew his horn at us, pissed off that we were blocking the road, and began yelling at us to hurry up.

Something in me snapped. I don't know if it was hearing someone yell at me the way my father used to, or if I was experiencing a fierce need to protect my wife and family that caused my anger to flare, but I lost my cool completely. You know those movies with the Incredible Hulk? The guy who rips off his clothes because he puffs up his shoulders and chest in fury? Yeah, that was me, all puffed up and furious, marching straight toward the cab driver, yelling, "Shut the fuck up, you *hijo de puta!*"

"Miguel, *calmate*, it's all right," Martina begged behind me, but I could barely hear her. All I could see was this prick trying to mow my family down.

When I reached the cab, I actually yanked the driver's door open and tried to pull him out, even more pissed off because the guy had the balls to laugh at me. Martina grabbed my arm and pulled me off him. "Come on," she said. "It's not worth it. Think of *el niños.*"

And with that, I snapped back into my own mind and body, stuffing that Transformer deep inside of myself again.

■ ■ ■

Although I was working most of every day, I devoted as many of my free hours as possible to the kids, giving them the kind of quality time I'd never had with either of my parents. I never yelled at them or spanked them, no matter how much mischief they made—and they made plenty.

Cristobal, especially, was a ball of nonstop energy, constantly asking questions and getting into trouble. He had such a strong will that he threw tantrums whenever he didn't get his way. I tried to be

Say Cheese

firm about limits while admiring his will. Tuti was a more easygoing child, gentle and sweet, though still nonstop work like all babies.

It was during this blissful time in my life that I received some tragic news: a friend of mine who had worked at the cheese factory with me in California called to say that Juan, my former boss, had shot himself.

All of the breath left my body, and I had to sit down. "*¿Que eres?* Why would he do such a thing?"

"The workers at his factory were threatening to unionize," my friend said sadly. "I guess Juan couldn't handle the pressure. They were breathing down his neck, and so were his brothers."

After we hung up, I sat for a long time, closing my eyes and remembering Juan's exuberant laugh. I thought of Pamela, too, and of Juan's children, and how hard it would be for them to grow up without a father. Juan and I hadn't shared the same values when it came to marriage, but I had considered him a friend. He must have felt so depressed and alone to do such a thing. I truly couldn't imagine his state of mind, surrounded as I was by work and family and love.

■ ■ ■

As the business continued growing, Martina started handling the invoices and other paperwork. I relied on her more and more as a partner. She was so tired from juggling this administrative work while caring for our baby daughter that I began bringing Cristobal in the cheese truck with me whenever I could. I made a bed for him in the truck so he could sleep while I was on the road and gave him toys he could play with when he was awake. When Cristobal was bored, I sang songs to keep him occupied. Though I knew this wasn't the best possible environment for my son, I was glad to have his company.

I was still logging many, many hours on the highway to visit with customers, drum up sales, and deliver cheese. One night, I was leaving Monroe with a semitrailer full of cheese and hit black ice. I eased up on the accelerator, but forgot to take the air brake off all the way. This was a near-fatal error. My stomach dropped as I glanced in the rear view mirror and saw the trailer hitched to my cab start fishtailing and nearly tip over. Fortunately, I released the air brake in time, and the truck righted itself. Still, terror caused bile to rise in my throat, and my heart hammered against my ribs. I was lucky it was three o'clock in the morning, and nobody else was on the road, so I was able to swerve into the other lane and bring the truck to a stop. I was fortunate, too, that Cristobal wasn't with me that time.

Another time, I was driving back to Monroe from Chicago when my vision blurred. It was as if someone had strapped a pair of binoculars to my face backwards; the road was like a funnel in front of me. I pulled over to the side of the highway, my heart racing like crazy, my breath coming in short, painful gasps, and clung to the dashboard. When I could breathe again, I drove myself straight to the nearest hospital emergency room.

They couldn't find anything wrong with me. "My guess is that you're suffering from stress and exhaustion," the doctor said. "Looks like you had an anxiety attack."

Still, I couldn't slow down. The sacrifices I was making were a gift for my family. I never wanted to go back to being poor. Even more importantly, now that I'd invested so much time and energy into cheese making, I wanted to keep pushing myself to see if I could succeed in turning my dreams into reality. I was determined to make a good living through straightforward, honest work to ensure that my children had everything I lacked. Besides, even if I wanted to slow down, it would have been difficult because Mr. Vega was still after me to send him more and more cheese.

Meanwhile, Webster and I continued working with the Amish to try and get them to improve the quality of the milk. We'd managed to institute a routine at the factory of washing the vats regularly to

105

Say Cheese

keep the milk as sanitary as possible, but I was still hesitant to try making the different cheeses Mr. Vega was starting to ask for, like queso fresco.

In producing the cotija cheese, I scraped the outer rind of each wheel to make it look more like cheese made in Mexico, figuring that would help out sales. One day, I decided to collect the shaved powdery cheese—it looked a lot like Parmesan—in plastic bags, thinking these cheese shavings might be perfect for customers who wanted powdered cotija to sprinkle on foods like roasted corn on the cob. "What do you think?" I asked Mr. Vega on my next trip to La Hacienda, holding up one of the bags. "Think you can sell powdered cotija cheese like this?"

"Oh yes. Nobody else is selling that product, Miguelito," he said, rubbing his hands together with enthusiasm. "You'd better bring me a whole semi load of this stuff. It's like gold!"

It was. I started bringing Mr. Vega not only the 60-pound wheels of cotija, but cotija powder, too, in 1- or 5-pound bags.

I was fortunate to be among the first cheesemakers to introduce Hispanic-style cheeses. The US marketplace was crowded with cheesemakers selling commonplace products like Cheddar and Monterrey Jack. That meant there were stringent FDA rules they had to follow to pass inspections, and they couldn't charge any more for their cheeses than their competitors. Nobody paid attention to Mexican cheeses at the time; there were no rules yet for consistency or formulas for moisture, fat, or anything else. Mexican cheeses weren't subject to market competition, either, because there just weren't enough people making them yet. My cotija wheels and powdered cotija were selling so briskly that Webster and I decided to register our company.

We didn't have the volume of goods or infrastructure to do our own distribution, but we hoped to sell our cheese to other brands that did. With that in mind, we decided on a name for our company that was general enough to cover anything we might want to do in the future: Mexican Cheese Producers. Martina, who had been tracking and processing our invoices and payments, helped us create a logo for our labels with a graphic designer in Ohio, and we were officially in business.

■ ■ ■

Within a year, Martina and I had enough money to leave our trailer and rent a nice house built by the Amish. It wasn't especially large or fancy, but the house was well-designed and hand built with wood; even the closets smelled like clean wood shavings. One night, we invited Webster and his wife, Annette, to dinner at our house along with some other friends. As we gave them the tour, showing them the various rooms and the generous yard, Annette grew increasingly pissed off and began picking fights with us, especially with Martina. Annette had always made it clear that she thought we were beneath her.

I had never trusted Annette, really, but I respected her because she was married to my best friend. After that night, though, I made it a point to see Webster on his own. I was too busy to have any patience for Annette's attitude toward us, which was a painful reminder of how I'd been treated by too many people for my lack of money and education—including Martina's own mother.

We were happy in that house, and I was finally beginning to feel settled. My hard work was starting to really pay off. Yes, we were a bit far from town, and there weren't a lot of Latinx immigrants in that part of Ohio, but my wife and children were safe and comfortable. That was everything to me, and I was grateful.

In a way, I was grateful to my father, too, for showing me the disastrous effects alcohol could have on a family. It pained me to see some of my own workers go down that same road. One of our cheesemakers, Joey, was a wonderful worker and a great guy, but he rarely drove his car without a six-pack of beer beside him. One day

Say Cheese

he got behind the wheel after he'd been drinking and disappeared in a heavy snowstorm.

When two days had passed without him showing up for his shift, we called his parents and the police to find out if he'd had an accident or been taken ill. Nobody knew where he was. It wasn't until six months later, when the snow finally melted, that the police found Joey's car in a local pond, where it had sunk, nose-down, through the ice.

■ ■ ■

One day, I was delivering cheese to Mr. Vega at La Hacienda when I ran into Jose Ortiz. He was a tall, skinny guy with curly hair and a huge mustache. He worked as a driver for La Hacienda, delivering products to stores in New York and New Jersey.

"Is it tough to break into the East coast market?" I asked.

Jose laughed. "No, man, there's like a million *Mexicanos* living in that area. Come with me next time, and I'll show you where to go."

Jose delivered up to five semitruck loads of Mexican products of all kinds to the East Coast each week. He introduced me to some of his customers as we navigated a dizzying maze of highways and city neighborhoods choked with people and traffic.

My goal was to make the cheese deliveries myself to some of these customers to cut out any middlemen. Taking the truck into New York on my own was a terrifying experience. Back then, there was no such thing as being able to navigate with GPS on your cell phone, so I had to rely on talking to other truck drivers on the CB radio for directions. Slowly, with many wrong turns, I made my way into Queens and the Bronx, and even into some New Jersey cities with high percentages of Latinx immigrants. Always, I sought out the person who controlled most of a particular market; for instance, I sold cheese through distributors like New York Produce and La Abarrotea.

Still, the driving took too much of a toll on me, and eventually I gave up and hired Jose to deliver our cheese, too.

The East Coast provided us with a seemingly infinite market. The pace of my life continued to escalate. It was like pushing a boulder up hill and feeling it crest and begin rolling down the other side. I didn't want to ever fail my family, my company, or my customers, so I ran right alongside that boulder, keeping up as best I could.

Of course, looking back now, I wish once again that I had stopped to take a breath, to play with my children and enjoy the success I had, rather than continuing to run until it felt like my heart might give out. That's the all-or-nothing essence of entrepreneurship that every business owner has to learn to balance. It would take me many more years before I'd find that balance in my life. Ironically, I'd have to lose everything before I realized how much I actually had to treasure in my own life.

Meanwhile, I was pushing myself to be a little better every day. Even 1% better than yesterday was still a step forward.

Part III

LIVING THE AMERICAN DREAM

Chapter 7

Expulsion and Reinvention

Our Most Important Lessons Can Come from Unexpected Teachers.

I admired a great deal about the Amish community, particularly their commitment to a simple, no-frills lifestyle and their dedication to helping each other. For instance, if someone fell ill, the entire community stepped in to assume that person's responsibilities and take care of their health needs. And when one of the barns burned down, the Amish gathered to build a new one for that farmer within days. On the other hand, they were stuck in their ways and determined not to change. Our biggest problem turned out to be milk supply. Webster and I were already having trouble making enough cheese to meet Mr. Vega's orders, and now we had an even larger market to tap on the East Coast. I calculated that we could easily use at least 300,000 pounds of milk a day—twice the amount we were currently receiving from our Amish partners.

One day, I went to them with a proposition: What if they increased their milk production?

"I can buy any amount of milk you can produce," I explained, "and we'll all make a better living."

This idea wasn't in keeping with their lifestyle, apparently, because our Amish partners almost immediately told Webster that he needed to get rid of me. "We have no intention of expanding," they said. "We need to maintain things the way they are. Either Miguel goes, or we'll shut down the operation."

"If Miguel goes, then I go," Webster replied, determined to call their bluff.

But the joke was on us. "Fine," they said. "You have a month to get out of our factory. We'll find another cheesemaker."

And just like that, Webster and I were essentially blacklisted by the Amish for being too ambitious. I was in shock. I'd literally put myself out of business without a Plan B. What now?

■ ■ ■

After our Amish partners gave us a firm deadline to be out of the factory within a month's time, I woke up most mornings in a panic. How were we going to live? I could barely look Martina in the eye because I didn't want her to know how worried I was about providing for our family. It felt like the walls of our home were closing in on me.

So I turned to the only skill I had to save us: cheese making. I switched over the factory to make cincho cheese and stockpiled it so we'd have something to sell after we could no longer use the Amish factory. Cincho is made with semi-skim cow's milk, rennet, and salt, and it has a grainy, firm texture. It has to be aged to mature, usually for at least four months, so it was the perfect cheese to make and keep in a refrigerated warehouse as an investment we could draw on in the future.

Webster and I worked day and night to produce an inventory of 80,000 pounds of cincho cheese. Meanwhile, we began looking around in the area—somewhat desperately, given our tight deadline—for a new opportunity.

Within a couple of weeks, Webster had worked his contacts to find us an old factory in Darlington, Wisconsin, that we could buy for $60,000. The factory had belonged to a company that used to make Parmesan and Swiss cheese for Kraft before it closed. Then we went to Darlington Dairy Supply to plead our case: if they would loan us equipment and install it in our new building on credit, we'd pay them back over time once we were up and running.

"We'll pay you back even faster if things go well," I said. "With interest, of course."

We had been dealing with the owners of this company for years, starting when we were at Klondike and selling equipment for them that was no longer viable to use in the United States, so we considered these people friends as well as business colleagues. To our relief, they agreed. We had always been honest with them, and now that honesty led them to believe in me and in our business, so they were willing to advance us the credit we needed to start our business.

Next, we had to deal with the problem of milk suppliers. This meant going to a bank and applying for a loan—the first I'd ever needed. Fortunately, I also had the cincho cheese I'd made and stored, which I now sold to a guy who had a small warehouse in his garage. That gave us enough cash to help keep our milk supply steady. We were officially in business again.

■ ■ ■

My mother rarely came north to see us, but when she said she wanted to help us move from Ohio to Wisconsin, I happily bought her a ticket. At one point, I was driving some of our boxes to our new home when we passed by a highway sign for the University of Notre Dame in Indiana.

"That's where my *padre* went!" she said excitedly. "Your *abuelo* got his engineering degree there."

I glanced at her. "Really? I didn't know that."

"Yes. He talked about how happy he was. He'd gone to high school in California and then studied there before he came back to *México* to run the *rancho* and start his factory."

I thought about this as we continued on to Wisconsin. "We should go see Notre Dame sometime," I said impulsively.

"Really?" My mother was startled; it was rare that anyone offered to do things for her.

"*Sí*, of course. It's an important part of our family history. Let's go."

We had a great visit. I was proud to show my mother our new home in Monroe and the factory in Darlington and to have her understand that I was becoming well-established financially. My only regret was that my father wasn't here to see what I'd accomplished. He'd never believed I was capable of doing anything.

I couldn't help thinking back to the time I'd helped him sell drinking water and about the arguments we'd had. One of the biggest was over my father's insistence that he should deliver the water to customers himself. Even though I was only a child, even I could see it would have made much more strategic and financial sense for him to hire someone at a low wage to deliver the water, while he went out and made customer calls to drum up business.

"You need to hire people to be more efficient," I'd told him.

"You don't fucking know anything, kid," was my father's response every time I tried to give him advice.

He was a dreamer, a stupid man who never could figure out the sequence of steps to create a successful business. Thank God I was nothing like him.

The following week, I took my mother and Martina on a road trip to the University of Notre Dame. We drove through the tree-lined campus and parked near the main administration building, a Gothic-looking stone building topped with a gold dome and statue.

"I can't believe *Abuelo* was lucky enough to study and live here," I said. "It's *hermoso*."

My mother was quiet beside me, but when I looked at her, I could see that her eyes were shining with tears. "I still miss him," she said softly.

Inside the building, a receptionist greeted us warmly. When she asked the reason for our visit, my mother spoke up, and I translated.

"She'd like to know if you have any records of my grandfather being here," I said.

"Let me see what we can do," the receptionist said.

Minutes later, another woman joined us from the alumni office. She asked us questions about my grandfather's field of study and what years he was here, then went off and began digging through the records. Within minutes, we had a transcript showing my grandfather's coursework and grades.

By then, I was nearly crying with excitement, too. Not so much because we'd found hard evidence of my grandfather being here, but because my tiny mother, who had struggled so hard and for so long in her life, was weeping openly at the sight of her father's name on these official papers. It was clear to me at that moment, as it had never been before, just how much my mother had adored her father, and how loved he'd made her feel. She'd had a happy childhood, and I was glad of that. She'd certainly had little enough joy in her life after that. At least I could give her this happy moment.

On the way home, I thought about all of this. My mother had been—and still was—a beautiful woman. She'd grown up in a wealthy, loving, well-educated family and had given up on the idea of going to college to marry my father, the handsome, charismatic son of a military doctor. Women were expected to marry and become wives and mothers back then. This should have been a good match for both of them.

Instead, my father was a barbarian, a man who had transformed himself with drink and took down everyone and everything in his path without remorse. From my father, I'd inherited some good things—my charm, my height—but I also feared the pride and anger that lurked inside me, and I'd worried that I might turn out to be as worthless a human being as he was.

From my mother's side of the family, I'd been granted creativity, the ability to solve problems logically, and the resilience to learn

117

Expulsion and Reinvention

from failure. I had to keep reminding myself of this sometimes, that I had more good things in me than bad.

■ ■ ■

While I'd been living in Mexico and Ohio, the demographics of Darlington, Wisconsin, had begun to change. More Hispanic immigrants—mostly from Mexico and other countries in Central America—had begun to settle in the Midwest, attracted by the promise of jobs. Many of the dairy farms were desperate for help since most US citizens, including their own children, refused to work on the farms.

The reality is that the dairy industry in Wisconsin would collapse without Latinx immigrant laborers. Around 2004, the state began increasing its milk production every year. It has set records almost every year since, largely because of export sales. That means there aren't enough American-born workers to fill the jobs. At one point while I was building my cheese factory, immigration officials came in and picked up all of the illegal immigrants in our area's dairy farms. Not surprisingly, the cows started dying because there weren't enough people to milk them or clean out the barns. It wasn't long before the government officials had to let immigrants go back and work on the farms.

A survey taken by the National Milk Producers Federation in 2014—the most recent one available—shows that more than half of the workers on dairy farms are immigrants from Latin America. Most are Mexican. These entry-level jobs offer more money than immigrants can make back in their homelands and often include modest housing. The work is difficult, even grueling and dangerous. Often dairy farms expect 10-hour days, even seven days a week. However, like me, these immigrants are willing to work hard because they see their jobs on Wisconsin farms as a ladder to a brighter future.

Webster and I only needed about 35 employees to run the factory in the beginning, but we still had difficulty filling those jobs.

The House that Cheese Built

We were desperate enough to rehire Jeff, the man who'd tried to knife me in my sleep all those years ago. Then Jose Ortiz, who was still delivering cheese for me, introduced me to some of his friends from the Chicago area, other Mexican immigrants who were looking for work.

These men brought in others to work for us, mostly from Mexico, El Salvador, and Honduras. Prospective employees showed me their papers, and I hired them without asking too many questions. I needed employees, just like all of the dairy farms and other factories around me. Besides, I understood their struggles back home and knew I could trust them to work hard for me so they could send money to their families.

■ ■ ■

Now that there was no limit on the amount of milk I could use at the factory, Webster and I upped our cheese production even more. As the number of semis driving in and out of the factory escalated, one of our neighbors—the man who owned the house next to our factory—began complaining about the noise and activity. One night, he ran outside with a chain saw, so drunk he slurred his words and swayed from side to side. The workers were alarmed enough to call me.

When I showed up, the neighbor was shouting, "I'm going to cut down all of your fucking electrical poles!" and revving up the chain saw.

"Please don't do that," I said. "I don't want to have to call the police."

"I don't care what you do, you fucking Mexicans! I'm cutting off your electricity right now!"

"Go ahead," I said. "We'd love to sue you. But I have a better idea. Why don't you sell us your house? We'd be happy to buy it from you. That way, you can go live somewhere quieter. How much do you want for it?"

The man was surprised enough to turn off his chain saw. "What the fuck did you say?"

"I said we could buy your house so you could move somewhere quieter. How much do you want for it? Forty thousand?"

"Fuck, it's worth more than that!"

He was right. It was worth twice that much, if only to get this guy out of my hair, so I paid him $80K the next day. This turned out to be a brilliant idea. We now had a place to house our Mexican workers so they could save money on rent and walk to work. We built a basketball court outside the factory and a park, too, so the employees would have somewhere to spend their free time. We promised they wouldn't have to pay any rent as long as they worked on the production line and completed their shifts.

After watching me stand up to that guy and argue him into selling me his house, the workers started calling me "El Gallo," which means "The Rooster." They didn't have to explain that nickname to me; growing up, I'd been to many cockfights, where the roosters were often pitted against each other to fight for money, often with tiny lethal metal spurs attached to their legs. The roosters never conceded, no matter how outmatched they were. They always fought to the death.

■ ■ ■

By now, Mexican Cheese Producers was stocking the store shelves all over Chicago, New York, and New Jersey. The only problem was that, because many of our clients were immigrants themselves, they tended to mistrust banks. They kept their money hidden at home and paid us in cash.

One day, I showed up at the bank in Darlington, Wisconsin, with about $180,000 cash to deposit, and the manager came out to greet me. "Mr. Leal," he said, shaking my hand, "please step into my office for a moment if you will."

The House that Cheese Built

I followed him inside with my thick envelopes of bills and sat down in front of his desk. He stood behind it and shook his head. "Look, we love having your business, we really do," he said, "but I have to ask you to stop making these huge cash deposits."

"Why?" I didn't see the problem.

"It's just a matter of bookkeeping," he assured me. "We need you to tell your customers to write checks from now on."

I was hesitant, but I went home to explain things to Martina. To my surprise, she agreed with the bank manager, saying, "*Mira*, Miguel, the truth is that it would be terrible if you were in the truck and got robbed, right? How would you even prove you had that much cash if somebody stole it? Or if the *policia* stopped you, they'd probably think you were doing something illegal if they saw all that money in the truck with you."

"But what do we do?" I asked. "A lot of our *clientes* don't even have checkbooks." The truth was that, coming from Mexico and the type of family I had, I understood this. I wasn't altogether comfortable with banks and government agencies, either. There was too much corruption in Mexico for the average person to trust anybody.

"I will teach them *que hacer*," Martina declared, and she did, giving our clients blank checks and helping them fill in the numbers.

It's a good thing she did, too, because our business continued to skyrocket as we expanded, selling our cheeses in more states. The first year Mexican Cheese Producers was in business, we jumped from processing 200,000 pounds of milk to 600,000 pounds. The potential to go even bigger was definitely there if we could expand our reach.

We were in exactly the right place at the right time. New York had been the top-producing cheese state at the turn of the twentieth century, but Wisconsin took that title in 1910, with a cheese factory for every 2.8 square miles in Green County, Wisconsin. By the middle of the twentieth century, there were seven distinct regions of cheese production in Wisconsin, thanks to the continued influx of people immigrating to the United States. They represented almost every country in Europe; many chose Wisconsin because of its reputation for cheese making, and they arrived with a desire to continue the tradition of making popular cheeses from the old country.

By the time I began making cheese, improved breeding and livestock nutrition in Wisconsin had resulted in large increases in the quality and quantity of the milk supply: approximately 11,000 dairy farms with 1.27 million cows produced an average of 21,436 pounds of milk annually. Wisconsin cheesemakers were using 90% of this milk supply to produce more than 2.8 billion pounds of cheese at 126 plants and had more skilled cheesemakers than any other state.

■ ■ ■

Within three years, we'd reached maximum production capacity at the factory in Darlington, turning upward of 400,000 pounds of milk a day into cheese. Naturally, this level of production required a lot of cleaning to ensure the cheese remained free of contamination, and we were starting to have trouble with the sewer lines backing up from all of the water and cheese residue running through the pipes. City officials pressured us to move farther out of town.

"What do you think, Miguel?" Webster asked. "Can we handle another move?"

"If we move, we can keep expanding," I said.

"Is that what you want to do?"

For once, I was the one who hesitated. I was already working 12-hour days, often seven days a week. How much more could I do? Martina never complained about how hard I worked, but I was missing a lot of valuable time with the children, who seemed to be taller and older every time I walked through the front door.

On the other hand, Webster and I were definitely on a roll. I'd already begun designing a new grinder for the cotija cheese, one that would further automate production and make it faster and safer. This was our chance not only to expand our operation, but to build a new factory from the ground up and design it so that it was more efficient than the one we'd bought and rehabbed.

And so we went for it. Webster and I shopped around for property nearby so we could keep our terrific working relationship with the people at Darlington Dairy Supply and the area farmers, who all belonged to different dairy cooperatives that delivered milk to us. Eventually, we settled on a piece of land, where we built a factory 10 times bigger than the one we'd been occupying. This was larger than we needed at the time, but we hoped to grow into it. I felt confident that I knew the market and the taste of the immigrant community.

Starting over from the ground up allowed me to design the production floor and install equipment that would increase our automation, efficiency, and sanitary practices, thus ensuring we could produce more cheese without having to hire a lot more workers. In our new factory, we could run through a million pounds of milk a day. I expected that to be our full capacity, and anticipated that it would take a long time to reach it.

I was wrong.

■ ■ ■

Once we had the new factory up and running, I decided it was time to start expanding into new territory. It made sense to produce fresh cheese—queso fresco—and panela next, since I had these recipes nearly perfected from working with Juan in California. Still, I would have to tweak them to accommodate the slightly different flavor and higher quality of Wisconsin milk versus the milk we had been using in California. I also wanted to make doubly sure that we were putting cheese on the market that would be free of potentially harmful bacteria.

I experimented with the recipes over and over again to perfect them, making small batches at a time and testing the product. Fortunately, my friend Hector Obregon—the chemical engineer I'd first met in Mexico, who had helped me develop the method of flash-freezing cheese in a steel tunnel with carbon dioxide when I was in Don Poncho's factory—was now working in a laboratory in Madison, Wisconsin. I went there and asked the people at the lab to help me test my queso fresco recipe while I kept adjusting it. The recipe I made here had to be created not only for Wisconsin's grade A milk, but also for the different winter and summer seasons, because cows produce milk with more fat content in winter than they do when they're grazing outside in the summer.

Eventually I hit on the perfect recipes for both queso fresco and panela. I was still painstakingly careful about keeping the cheese free of bacteria; I remembered all too well the tragedy of those 60-some people who had died after eating contaminated fresh cheese made by Jalisco. Any time we took returns from stores because of spoiled cheese, I'd take the returned products back to Hector's lab to be tested so I could understand how and why coliform bacteria had adulterated them. Coliform bacteria occur naturally in surface water, soil, and in the intestines of mammals; fortunately, most of it isn't harmful. (The big exception is E. coli, which comes from fecal waste and can be fatal to humans.)

It didn't take long to determine that, as long as we trained the workers to clean the equipment thoroughly every four hours, that eliminated any contamination. I also froze the cheese in a carbon dioxide tunnel immediately upon production.

Within a few months, we were able to deliver our first batches of panela and queso fresco to Mr. Vega. Sales skyrocketed immediately. The products flew off our shelves faster than we could produce them, as the big-box stores and restaurants that catered to clients from Latin America—like Sam's Club, Walmart, Taco Bell, and others—began buying our cheeses. I needed to figure out a way to produce fresh cheese faster and pondered this problem until I hit on a novel solution.

In Mexico, queso fresco is sold in rounds; the rounds are formed by putting the fresh cheese—which has the texture of thick paste—into stainless steel rings. The cheese rounds are then put into a cooler and packaged. Most Mexican factories have their workers do this by hand; it can be time consuming, but labor is cheap in Mexico.

Labor was costly in the United States, so I needed to come up with some kind of technological solution. I began touring other factories to look at their equipment, and when I visited McCormacks Meats factory outside of Chicago, I hit on the perfect solution: they had a machine that could make hamburger patties of different sizes. Why couldn't I do that with fresh cheese?

I bought one of those patty machines and started testing it. It was a round head with five pistons, and the deepest head, when filled with cheese, could churn out perfectly-shaped, 15-ounce rounds of cheese much faster than human hands.

There was just one problem: potential contamination. Webster and I remained focused on producing top-quality cheese and always put safety first. We hired Martina's older sister, Maria Louisa, to join us as head of quality control when we started making queso fresco. Maria Louisa was a chemist who'd majored in food science and was previously working for a food processing company in Mexico. Because of her expertise and the size of our company, it was easy for us to get her a work visa and bring her north.

I enjoyed having Maria Louisa around, though I can't say the employees embraced her presence. Maria Louisa was as no-nonsense as Martina when it came to work, and she did everything by the book. She ran our lab and made her presence known on the floor, checking to see that the employees were keeping things scrupulously clean, and testing every vat of queso fresco for salmonella, listeria,

125

Expulsion and Reinvention

and coliforms. This was an essential part of cheese making. The biggest potential stumbling block to our success would be producing a batch of contaminated cheese that would make people sick; if that happened, my reputation and the business would both go to hell. I didn't want to risk anything that might put the public's safety or our company's future in danger.

Now that we were selling more queso fresco, we were also getting more calls from customers who wanted to return the cheese because it was contaminated with bacteria. What happens with contaminated cheese that has been vacuum-packed, as our was, is that the cheese starts producing gas as it warms, so the plastic around it begins to inflate. We took each bad batch of cheese to the lab at the University of Wisconsin to have it tested; fortunately for us, the contamination was caused by coliform bacteria that wasn't harmful to humans, but I was still wary and determined to find a way to keep our cheese clean.

The solution turned out to be simple: we had to train the workers to thoroughly wash and rinse the patty machine every four hours. And, before long, we found even more efficient equipment to replace the patty machine we'd originally retrofitted. The new machine was one I'd seen at a trade show and was designed to make hamburgers by squeezing the meat through a tube using pressure, then cutting it up into patties at top speed.

FDA regulations would prevent me from using this exact machine, but I bought one and had a team of engineers at Faith Engineering retrofit it for my factory, using a jacket of carbon dioxide so the cheese rounds would be frozen as they emerged. The machine could cut six or seven rounds of queso fresco in a single section, each of them at the exact weight we set it for, without a single pair of hands touching them. I suggested to Jim Faith that we also add a spiral tunnel infused with carbon dioxide, the way I'd frozen cheese in Mexico, so that by the time the cheese was delivered into the packaging machine, it was frozen. It was wrapped before any of the workers put the cheese into boxes for shipping.

Once we were selling queso fresco and panela cheese as well as cotija, our sales took another leap forward. I was pleased, but not at all shocked by our meteoric rise in the marketplace. I was the only Mexican cheesemaker who was specializing in Hispanic-style cheese; I was purposefully targeting stores where Mexican people shopped in the United States; and I knew what these immigrant communities craved.

A number of these companies approached me with offers to have me sell my products exclusively to them. The products would then continue going out under their brand names. This was tempting, given the financial incentives, but Webster and I declined. We were afraid to put all of our eggs in one basket and give up control of our products.

■ ■ ■

Like most immigrants, I was worried about my family back home. My brothers were all older than I was but less successful. As I became increasingly busy with ramped-up production at the factory, I decided that I needed someone else to share the burden. One of the jobs I hated most was driving the delivery truck; if I could spend less time on the road, I'd see my children more often at dinner and be able to devote some daylight hours to testing out new recipes. My brother Jose was working as an accountant in El Paso, Texas. Pedro was aimless but had married into a good family and was working with Carlos. My brother Joaquin was the one I worried about the most; he was a heavy drinker and had no direction at all. I decided to give him a call to see if he'd be willing to come north and take over my delivery route. He agreed at once.

I devoted six months to training Joaquin, taking him on the road with me to teach him the route and introduce him to our customers.

Expulsion and Reinvention

It was wonderful to be with him again, and I loved the idea that Joaquin would now have a purpose in life and a steady paycheck.

During our long drives, we reminisced about our childhood while we navigated the roads and dropped off cheese to my customers. "Never, ever miss a *gasolina* station on the highway if your tank is even half empty," I reminded Joaquin several times. "If you don't put diesel in this truck and keep it running, you'll freeze your *huevos* off out here by yourself on the highway, especially late at night when there's nobody to rescue you. The weather here is nothing like Mexico's."

Finally, I felt he knew the route and customers well enough to make the deliveries on his own. "Okay, *mi hermano*," I said finally. "You're ready to go solo."

Things seemed to go smoothly at first, other than one occasion where I received a phone call from another driver saying he'd passed Joaquin's truck pulled over by the side of the road. "He says he forgot to put diesel in the truck," my friend told me.

I pulled on my clothes and drove with a can of diesel out to Route 80, where I found Joaquin shivering with his kid and wife in the truck. It was below zero degrees. "*Jesuchristo*, man, what did I tell you, keeping at least half a tank of diesel in the truck?" I scolded. "This isn't Mexico. You could freeze to death out here if you're not careful! You're just lucky my *amigo* saw you."

A few weeks later, I received a furious call from Mr. Vega. "Miguel, are you trying to undercut my business?"

"What are you talking about?" I clutched the phone, terrified by his tone. In all of the time I'd been selling cheese to him—over two years, now—I'd never seen Mr. Vega lose his temper.

"One of my customers has boxes of your cheese, *hombre*, and since that *queso* didn't come from my warehouse, it must have come from yours. He says he bought it for two dollars a pound! What the *chingados* is going on? Are they stealing that cheese from you or from me?"

My stomach felt heavy with dread. I understood at once what must have happened: my idiot brother Joaquin was going behind my back, skimming cheese out of my warehouse to sell on the sly so he could keep the profit for himself.

"*No se preocupe*, Mr. Vega," I said. "I will fix this."

I gave Joaquin $20K and sent him packing to Mexico the next day.

This was always the way with my brothers: they would always choose the path of least resistance in an attempt to get rich, even if it involved cheating strangers, each other, or the government. On another occasion, my brother Pedro came to Wisconsin in tears because he was certain the Mexican government was about to throw him in jail.

"*¿Porque?* What have you done?" I asked.

Carlos was living in Atlanta, Georgia, at the time. He and Pedro, who was living in Mexico, had started an import-export business. Carlos would buy denim seconds—denim fabric with small flaws— from manufacturers in the southern United States and ship it across the border to Pedro, who sold the fabric to factories in Mexico. This had been a modestly successful endeavor. Now the problem was that Pedro had been greedy or stupid, or maybe both, and hadn't paid any taxes to the Mexican government. He'd gotten caught, and the government was on his ass to pay up what he owed.

"They're going to put me in jail, Miguel," Pedro cried. "I lied to them, and now I don't have the *dinero* to pay the taxes." He was the most Catholic of my brothers and had brought his bible with him from Mexico; he wandered through our house, alternating between weeping and reading biblical passages to comfort himself. "What am I going to do, Miguel? I can't pay, I'm telling you. I just don't have the *dinero*. I can't pay!"

"Well, you can't run away from the *problema*, Pedro," I said. "You have to fix this. You're going to have to pay the taxes. Talk to Carlos and tell him the truth."

Expulsion and Reinvention

They sorted out the tax problems, but soon after that, they fought and abandoned the company. By the time Carlos moved back to Mexico, he was totally broke and came to me for help.

"I have a great idea for a new business," he told me.

I listened warily. Carlos said he wanted to buy the sort of fancy white tent that can be used for outdoor weddings and parties. "If you put up the *dinero*, Miguel, I can rent the tent out and go around putting it up for events," he said. "I'll pay you back, I swear. All I need is $45,000 to get started."

It didn't seem like a totally crazy idea, and Carlos and I had been through so much together that I couldn't refuse him. We bought the tent in Mexico and some carpets, too, so that the tent would look even nicer.

After a few months went by without hearing from him, I flew down to Mexico to check on Carlos and his business. To my shock, I discovered that Carlos had divorced his wife and was seeing another woman. Even worse, he'd started living in the tent himself! He'd sold all of his belongings and was now homeless, selling bread on the street to make enough money to feed himself and his new girlfriend.

I couldn't understand the division between my brothers and me. We were raised by the same parents, in the same circumstances, yet they felt like strangers to me in many ways. When my brothers failed at something, they blamed everything but themselves and turned to God for comfort. When I failed, I tried to learn from my mistakes and push forward. I pushed hardest of all when I was afraid; by now, I'd learned to trust myself to analyze my mistakes and do things better. If I wasn't scared, I figured I probably wasn't learning anything new. It might not have been my destiny to become a cheesemaker, but since that's what I had become, now I was determined to work hard and do it as successfully as possible.

Feeling so different from my brothers brought back that melancholy sense of having been cast adrift. Thank God I had Martina, who had known and loved me since we were children, or I would have felt completely alone.

■ ■ ■

By the time Cristobal was six and Tuti was three years old, we were all legal citizens of the United States, and I finally felt secure enough financially to buy a pretty Swiss-style chalet in Monroe so Cristobal could start school there. It was a two-story house in the center of town across the street from a church. The streets were wide and tree-lined and, most importantly, safe. We began buying furniture for the first time in our lives and met our neighbors, who all seemed friendly, though I worked too many hours to ever really get to know them closely. And for the first time, we bought a dog, a yellow lab named Max who delighted the kids and Martina.

That Christmas, we flew to Mexico for the first time in five years. Our daughter, Tuti, was a US citizen because she'd been born here, but it had taken that long for Martina and Cristobal to be granted citizenship. Looking at my wife and children on the plane, I felt so grateful that we were American citizens and succeeding in our new lives, but I was also committed to showing my children that they were Mexican, too. I vowed to make sure they knew our customs and extended family.

It was a joyful reunion. We spent most of our vacation on the farm with Martina's parents, her sisters, and their families. My father-in-law killed a bull for a grand cookout, and many of my family members came, too, and spent the night. We celebrated the occasion with fireworks, and my children got to hear many family stories from their grandparents. We also toured the nearby pyramids and ruins, Cañada de la Virgen, in San Miguel de Allende, an Otomi archaeological site that dates back to 530 AD. I was fascinated by this history, but of course the kids were more enthusiastic about learning to bash piñatas open with sticks and gathering candy from the ground.

Despite their young ages, my children were acutely aware that Mexico was not like the United States. They stared with wide eyes at the shacks many people lived in, the barefoot kids, the skinny dogs and cats, and the litter on the streets. At one point, Cristobal pinched his nose shut and said, "Why does it stink so bad? I'm glad we don't live here, Dad!"

I tried to explain about the poverty and told them that was why I'd left, to give them a better future in the United States, but they couldn't really absorb it. They were young, or maybe it's impossible for people of any age to really understand what it means to be poor unless they've struggled themselves. That's why so many politicians are out of touch with what people really need around the world: education, a roof over their heads, medical care, food to eat, and jobs to give them hope and grant them dignity.

To a casual observer, my home state of Guanjuato might appear calm and prosperous. US tourists and retirees gravitate to artsy San Miguel de Allende there, and major car manufacturers like Toyota, General Motors, and Mazda have brought jobs to the area. But poverty is a fact of life for too many Mexican citizens, and the violence continues to escalate as a result.

When I was a kid, I was surrounded by violence, starting close to home with my father. Memories still surfaced whenever I visited Mexico, even as a father and businessman. For instance, I remembered one nightmare Christmas where I traded my toys with a neighbor kid for his BB gun, and my father accused Joaquin of stealing the gun. He was drunk, of course, and began beating Joaquin so hard that everyone had to intervene to pull him off my brother.

I wasn't the only one of my childhood friends who'd grown up with violence, either. Once, I went to Chihuahua on a deer hunting trip with my friend Rodolfo. We were sitting in the car, eating radishes for a snack while his father went into the bank. When his father backed the car out of the bank parking lot, he hit the car behind him. Not surprisingly, that driver—a guy in a nice tie and suit—was pissed off. He got out of his car and came around to the driver's side, yelling at Rodolfo's dad, who pulled the guy through the window by his collar and stuck a pistol in his mouth.

"Don't fuck with me. I will kill you if you keep yelling at me!" Rodolfo's father screamed, and smashed the guy's teeth with his pistol. Then he shoved the guy to the ground and drove off with us silent and wide-eyed in the back seat. The scariest thing was that Rodolfo's father never expressed any regrets; his face was completely devoid of expression.

Violence begets violence, and in Mexico there was a lot of it. It has continued to escalate. For instance, in 2017, a local mob boss in my state known as "El Marro" (Sledgehammer) allegedly began stealing more than a million dollars' worth of fuel every day from the pipelines of a government-owned oil refinery. We already had a heavy-hitter trying to control everything in Guanajuato. That guy, whose nickname was "El Mencho," led the Jalisco New Generation cartel.

The trouble between El Mencho and El Marro broke out when the two began fighting over the lucrative drug trade. In July 2020, gunfire broke out at a neighborhood drug rehab center in my hometown of Irapuato, and 27 men died. This was just one more bloody episode in a wave of violence that has swept through my home state as this turf war continues to escalate. In 2018, my beloved Guanajuato earned the title of being Mexico's most violent state.

Even before this latest rash of violence, and despite my sadness at having raised children who are so culturally distant from my homeland, I feel certain I had made the best choice by immigrating to the United States. Nothing in Mexico will change until the broken political system is fixed, until less money goes to politicians and

Expulsion and Reinvention

people who are already wealthy and wriggling out of paying taxes, and more into the hands of struggling families who really need more money and support. I hope I live long enough to see those changes in my Mexico. Even more, I hope I can become part of the change.

I was resigned to the fact that my children were probably going to grow up speaking more English than Spanish, especially now that Cristobal was starting school, but I still wanted them to be fully aware—and proud—of being Mexican. At least I could take comfort in being in a position to help our family and friends. During this trip, one of my oldest friends, Octavio—the boy who had sheltered me when I thought my father might kill me—confessed that he was about to sell his father's gun collection to pay for his sister's surgery, which would cost the family $13,000.

I immediately gave Octavio the money. I never would have been able to forgive myself if he had sold all of his family's heirlooms and guns. Those weren't just objects, but priceless family memories—the kinds of memories I was trying to build with Martina and my children.

■ ■ ■

Because I was so busy with work, Martina handled the day-to-day childcare responsibilities when Cristobal and Tuti were young. I trusted her 100% to parent our children well. She was a good mother, and a firm one, seeing that they did their homework, ate well, and were involved in activities. Our children began developing their own friendships and competing in school sports. It made me happy, coming home in the evenings to this joyful home, to a loving wife and children who would never have to worry about where their next meal was coming from or whether they could buy new shoes for school.

The only hitch was that my children were growing further and further from my own language and culture. To compensate for this steady cultural evaporation, we brought a Mexican nanny, Lara, to help out with childcare, and I always spoke Spanish with them at home. I was pleased that Cristobal and Tuti both spoke Spanish fluently, not a "Spanglish" mix that many of my own factory workers used. We also traveled to Mexico a few times a year. We vacationed mainly with Martina's family; her father always made enormous bonfires and cooked outside to celebrate our homecomings. Other times we met up with my brothers and their families in Cancun and Puerto Vallarta.

I spent as much quality time with my children at home, too, attending games if they were competing on weekends. Martina arranged family vacations to Florida, New York, Canada, Belize, and other places where we could peel Cristobal and Tuti away from their friends and keep them close. I remained dedicated to being the kind of role model my father never was for me.

Martina and I did make a few good friends in Monroe, like Dale, an outgoing car salesman, and his wife, Dawn, whose children were friends with our kids. They introduced us to other people around town, and we often socialized and had parties together. Many times people were confused about my background and assumed I was European because of my height, blue eyes, and pale skin; in any case, I often felt left out of the conversations because I didn't understand their references to TV programs or many of their jokes. These were comfortable friendships, but nothing deep. I felt most comfortable holding serious conversations about business and investments.

For my own stress relief, I needed an adrenaline rush to help me relax. On one trip to Mexico with my extended family, when Cristobal was about seven and Tuti was four, I'd gone hang gliding with my cousin, Alejandro. I was instantly addicted to the rush of being towed up into the air behind a plane while strapped into a glider, then released to soar silently on thermal currents among the birds. As soon as we were back in Wisconsin, I found a small airport in

Whitewater that offered hang gliding lessons. The first lessons were in tandem with an instructor while I learned how to feel a thermal current and steer. Then I went up alone.

That first time by myself, I was terrified when the pilot of the small plane towing me signaled for me to let go. "Release, release!" he signaled over and over, as we hit one thermal current and then another and another, but I was too scared to do it. It must have taken 20 minutes before I finally got up the courage to unhook my tow rope from the plane.

Once released, I was instantly buoyed aloft by warm air currents and glided smoothly above the tidy green and yellow patchwork quilt of farm fields for over three hours. After that, I went back to Whitewater every weekend I could to repeat the experience. I'd never known anything like that sensation of floating in the air. In some ways, it was similar to scuba diving, in that it was quiet, the views were surreal, and I had the sensation of floating, but the adrenaline rush made it even more of a transformational experience. Hang gliding on weekends provided the ideal escape route from the tension I accumulated from the endless hours of my exhausting workweeks.

A couple of years later, Cristobal—who'd seen me hang gliding on several occasions—began begging me to let him go up, but I just couldn't do it, imagining him falling and being paralyzed or worse, dead, a pile of broken limbs on the ground. I could risk my own life and limbs for pleasure, but not my son's.

"Let's try something else, okay?" I said. "How would you like to learn how to ride a motorcycle?"

Now, when I look back on this idea of mine, I feel foolish. On what planet are motorcycles safe? But I was still relatively young and eager to take my boy out on special outings in ways my father had never done with me, so I bought a small dirt bike for Cristobal and a bigger one for myself. A friend of ours had created a dirt track with jumps on his farm, and I reasoned that, since we weren't riding on paved roads with cars, this would be a relatively safe way for us to burn some energy and get our thrills.

It was terrific fun, sailing over those jumps on a noisy dirt bike, but a few months after our new hobby began, I took a jump wrong, and the bike spun out. I lost control and landed beneath it. Thankfully, I emerged from the accident with nothing worse than bruised ribs, a bunch of scratches, a shattered ego—and a healthy respect for just how dangerous motorcycles could be even on dirt.

I didn't care about the danger for myself, but the thought of putting Cristobal in danger nearly crippled me with anxiety. We had to find a new hobby. Fortunately, Cristobal didn't have the same addiction to adrenaline; the accident scared him, too, and he didn't protest when I suggested selling the bikes.

■ ■ ■

Although we enjoyed living in Monroe, Martina and I were both tiring of the in-town location. We wanted more privacy, which meant buying more land. We found the perfect piece of property, about 22 acres not far outside of Darlington. One of my good friends, Bill, gave me some wise advice: "Miguel, you'd better let Martina build your house. Otherwise you'll exhaust yourself arguing over things like faucets and tile colors, and the project will take forever to finish."

So Martina worked with the architect and builder, and I mainly stayed out of the process, still devoting most of my waking hours to cheese production and distribution. When it was finished, our home was a gorgeous sprawling ranch situated in the middle of the property, with plenty of windows to let in light and let us watch the deer, turkey, rabbits, and other wild animals.

Martina seemed excited and happy, and watching her tackle this project and make a new home for us was enough to make me happy, too. Even though I could feel my children drifting away from their Mexican roots—they weren't interested in traditions like Day of the Dead and were beginning to resist traveling to Mexico, now that they were more invested in their own friendships and activities in the United States—Martina and I remained close. We talked about every aspect of the business, our home, and the children, and I considered her my best friend.

After we'd moved into our new home, the kids continued doing well in school and seemed to be busy every minute. Tuti was a competitive swimmer and had become a decent soccer player—she was always agile and a good athlete—and Cristobal was swimming and on the wrestling team, too. Both of them were popular. Cristobal, in particular, had my outgoing personality and was starting to socialize more now that he was in high school.

This is it, I thought. *We are living the American dream.*

I was convinced we were going to live happily ever after, just the way I had always pictured life with Martina. Sadly, I couldn't have been more wrong.

However, I was still learning essential lessons that would prove valuable both in continuing to expand my business and in the struggles to come when I would be threatened with a lawsuit and jail time. From the Amish, I had learned that supporting your own community could keep you strong, which was partly why I had decided to offer housing to the immigrants working in my factory after negotiating to buy the house from our unruly neighbor. And my business partners in Darlington had taught me that my honesty and good-faith working relationship with them could reap rewards, like a loan when I needed it to expand my business.

Building bridges in business is one of the surest ways to keep your network strong and vital enough for you to keep growing. You must prove yourself first and continue talking with people honestly about what you can—and can't—do for them, so they'll believe in your potential to deliver what you're promising. Whether the risk is financial or equipment, potential partners will only invest in your business after you build your personal brand by consistently demonstrating your work ethic, committing to making a great product, and delivering it in a timely fashion.

Chapter 8

Shooting Pigeons

Find Ways to Better Yourself Through New Education and Skills.

By the time Cristobal was 12, I was acutely aware that time was speeding by more quickly. Soon my son would be a teenager. If he was anything like me, he'd disappear and spend more time with his friends than with us, especially if he fell in love. I needed to make the most of our time together and create a father–son bond doing something that would endure through his adolescent passions.

"What would you think about learning to shoot a gun?" I asked one day.

He scoffed. "I already know how to do that from playing *Call of Duty*."

"Believe me, shooting a real gun is a lot different from shooting at targets in a video game. I'll sign you up for a safety course. You'll see."

"I don't need a safety course!" he protested.

"Sure you do. Everyone needs to know how to handle a gun safely," I said, adding, "That's how I met your mom, you know. During a shooting competition. I won money, and she was impressed."

He stared at me in disbelief. "You were actually good enough to win contests?"

"Good? I was a great shot!" I told him how, when I was a child, my Abuelo Pepe had taught me how to make slingshots out of old shoes, and all about Octavio's dad sponsoring me in competitions. "Maybe you're lucky enough to have inherited my ability."

"Maybe I'll even be better than you," Cristobal said.

I ruffled his hair. "Maybe, but you'll have to work hard to beat your *padre*."

"No contest," he insisted.

I bought Cristobal his first 20-gauge shotgun to settle that bet. Once Cristobal had completed his safety course, a cheesemaker I knew, John, invited us out to his gun club in Argyle. "Hey, you should take some shots, too, man," John said and loaned me his gun.

It had been a long time since I'd held a gun in my hands, but everything about shooting still felt completely natural to me. We were skeet shooting, and I shattered 48 targets out of 50 tries. Cristobal had definitely inherited my sure aim: he managed to shoot 37 clay pigeons out of 50 during his first time skeet shooting.

Cristobal was as excited as I was about our new sport. We bought more guns and equipment to practice with at home and worked our way up through the competitions to the Master Class level. We enjoyed it so much that, over the years, we began traveling to competitions, first locally, then nationally and internationally. Sometimes we competed individually and other times as a father–son team.

Learning to shoot, like learning to do most things well, takes some talent, but mostly requires many hours of practice and patience. Tuti, for instance, came with us a few times, but she had her mother's fatal flaw: for some reason, neither of them could close one eye and keep the other one open. Cristobal had a decent aim from the start. What he lacked was patience. For instance, during one practice session using an electronic rabbit that jumped instead of racing straight ahead, he missed it every time.

And every time he missed, my son would freak out. Eventually he turned to me in tears, whining, "What am I doing wrong? I can't get it, Dad!"

I led him away from the range and gave him a snack and a pep talk. "Sometimes in life, if you want something badly, it makes you nervous, and it's like your muscles get all tight," I said. "That throws off your aim. What you need to do is take deep breaths, relax, and pretend you don't give a shit. Because, really, the only person who cares if you hit that target is *you*."

This was one of the lessons I desperately wanted to teach my son: to trust himself first. Sure, you can ask people for advice, but in the end, only you can make the right decisions for your own life at any particular moment.

When we returned to the shooting range, I watched with pride as my son gathered himself, took deep breaths, and started shooting. This time he hit nearly every rabbit.

On another occasion, I taught Cristobal a different but equally important life lesson. We were in a competition, and Cristobal kept coming up to me and asking for advice, breaking my concentration.

"I don't know what I'm doing wrong, Dad," he said. "I keep missing!"

I was trying to focus because I really wanted to win this competition, so I was brusque with him. I turned around and snapped, "You know what? You're going to have to figure it out yourself this time."

He stomped off in a fury, but that anger served him well. From that day on, Cristobal was determined to be an even better shot than I was. More importantly, he'd learned that there are times when other people can't, or won't, teach him what he needs to do, and he needs to teach himself.

The point of entering shooting competitions for me was never about the money, though plenty of people offered to sponsor us, and there was usually prize money awarded to the winners. No, I was simply competing against my own personal best records, and shooting gave me a routine of discipline and training I could share with my son.

Shooting Pigeons

Part of that training meant taking him on hunting trips where he could shoot at real prey instead of clay pigeons. In Argentina, for instance, they were having a plague of pigeons. The birds were decimating the farmers' crops, sometimes eating up to 25% of the grain harvest, and there was an open call for hunters. Cristobal and I flew to Buenos Aires and then on to Cordoba. From there, we drove over two hours to a shooting lodge. It was wildly beautiful, and we reveled in the mountain air, fishing in the clean rivers whenever we weren't hunting birds.

Martina and Tuti often came along to cheer us on during our bigger competitions. The four of us traveled all over the country and to England, Spain, Portugal, and other countries where Cristobal and I were in tournaments. I grew increasingly passionate about the sport, which allowed me to be free, for those moments when I was shooting, of everything else in my life. There was no need to listen to anyone but myself to make the target. My capacity to react to the target and shoot at it with precision led me to feel alive and vital, especially as Cristobal and I climbed the ranks and represented the United States—my beloved adopted country—in international competitions. There was even talk among the sponsors of entering us into the Olympics.

Cristobal and I eventually competed in the Elite class, the highest level. We earned so many trophies that I had to add a room onto our house to accommodate them. Shooting gave us not only a physical outlet, but an emotional one, because the sport brought us together again and again, and each time, we had to set our egos and lives aside so we could focus on the moment. When you shoot a gun, you can only hit the target square if you shut out the whole rest of the world.

I was ecstatic, having these special times with my family. I never knew it was possible to be this happy. Yet, there were signs that not everything was as it seemed. My body picked up on these even though my mind refused to acknowledge the threat.

During one worldwide shooting competition, for instance, our family traveled to Oxford, England. Cristobal was 15 years old by then and Tuti was 12. Cristobal and I did well, earning a trophy as a father-and-son team, then our family took the train to France for some sightseeing. As the train rumbled along the tracks, the rest of my family fell asleep, but I found myself wide awake and suffering from the sensation that something was terribly wrong. I put a hand to my face and discovered it was damp; without knowing it, I had begun weeping, reacting to this sixth sense that something was very, very wrong with my family.

The feeling dissipated once we arrived in Paris. We toured so many art museums that my neck actually hurt from looking at paintings. Martina made us all laugh, jollying us along when we were tired, and the kids got along well. Still, something was telling me that things were not right.

■ ■ ■

After our trip to Europe, I continued having an odd feeling. Martina and I were doing all of the things we usually did—devoting most of our hours to work and otherwise spending time with the kids or taking an occasional overnight trip to Chicago—but something was definitely off. I couldn't pinpoint exactly what it was, but my wife wasn't acting like herself. She'd stopped kissing me in the mornings, for one thing, and she'd started wearing more makeup and dressing more provocatively.

My subconscious must have been obsessing over these changes because at one point I woke up at about three o'clock in the morning and sat bolt upright in bed, wide awake and fearful. I shook Martina's shoulder until she stirred and sat up, too.

"What is it?" she asked, pushing the hair out of her eyes. "*¿Que pasa?* Did you hear something?"

"Are you cheating on me?" I asked.

"*¿Que?* Why are you asking me this, Miguel?"

"I don't know. It's just this feeling I have that something's wrong."

She rolled her eyes at me and turned over, plumping the pillows beneath her head. "Go to sleep, for God's sake. You're being paranoid and talking *loco*."

I lay back down beside her, but couldn't seem to close my eyes. At that moment, my body was vibrating with tension, literally telling me I was sleeping with the enemy.

Despite the uneasiness in my marriage, during this time in my life, I learned to embrace the new discipline and skills I'd acquired through shooting competitions with my son. Developing prowess in my marksmanship required channeling my energy and developing many of the skills that made me sharper in the business world where, just as in shooting, being able to hit your mark takes practice, patience, and the ability to focus.

Chapter 9

One Last Cheese

To Achieve Success, Focus on One Goal at a Time.

When our new factory was fully up and running, Webster and I had the capability to run through a million pounds of milk every day. I'd thought that would be our capacity, but within a year we'd hit that mark, and it was clear we could produce more.

"We're going to need more space to give our customers what they want, Miguel," Webster said one day, "unless you want to dial things back a bit."

"I don't want to slow down," I declared. "Not yet. Let's expand the factory."

And so we did. With the help of a loan of $600,000 from my friend Mr. Vega, we were able to add another 10,000 square feet of space. This meant we now had the space to produce what I saw as the next logical product for the clients we served: crema Mexicana. This wasn't cheese, of course, but it was a dairy product I knew the Latinx community craved. Crema is typically sold in squeeze bottles around Mexico, where it provides a tangy accent to so many dishes, much the way people in the United States use sour cream as a condiment.

The main difference between the two is fat content. Crema has a higher fat content, about 30%, while sour cream's fat content is usually only around 20%. The other difference is that sour cream has thickeners and stabilizers added during the process, while Mexican crema is made without. Crema is less acidic, too, and tastes sweeter and saltier than sour cream. In my lab, I played around with recipes until I created a product similar to the thick, creamy liquid sold in bottles all over Mexico.

And, once again, our product was an instant success.

Mexican Cheese Producers (MCP) continued to grow, and Webster and I began seeking recognition for our work through various trade shows and contests. For instance, our 5-pound wheel of queso fresco was absolutely beautiful to look at, a white cheese with a creamy taste. It was like a bleu cheese without the bleu, if that makes sense. We entered that particular product in various contests, including the World Cheesemaking Contest, and took home many blue ribbons.

What this meant, of course, was that other, larger food production companies began to sit up and take notice of MCP. We were playing in the big leagues now, and several companies approached, interested in buying us out. None of the early offers appealed to me, though, either because I didn't like the people or the money they offered.

"You can't keep working at this pace, Miguel," Martina said at one point. "We never see you. Do you really want to keep up these hours, these long *dias* and weeks at work, for the rest of your life?"

"No, *claro que no*," I said.

"Before you know it, the kids will be out of the house, off living their own lives," she said. "You'll miss all of it, if you don't start slowing down. Don't we have enough *dinero*?"

It was one of the only times we'd ever argued. Throughout the many years we'd been married, Martina and I had seldom fought about anything. When it came to the business, I ran every idea past her because I respected her opinions. If she disagreed with me, she might say so, or she might ask questions, but I never lost my temper. That's why this somewhat heated discussion got under my skin.

Was Martina right? Was it time for me to sell the business and spend more leisure time with my family?

It was true that we already had plenty of money. We had a nice home, college funds for the kids, money for vacations, and decent savings. Martina and I had always been frugal.

It was also true that money—beyond being able to provide well for my family, that is—really didn't matter much to me. I drove the same kind of Ford pickup truck I'd always had and didn't care about clothes or fancy dinners. In fact, Martina bought most of my clothes, simply because I couldn't be bothered to shop. She was in charge of our personal finances, too; I didn't really even know how much money we had, only that we had plenty of it.

What did matter to me, then, if not making money? What was driving me forward to keep testing recipes and growing the company?

The answer was easy: challenging myself to always do better. Just as I competed to be the best shot possible when I held a rifle, I brought that same intensity to work, focusing on hitting one goal at a time. "Winning," to me, didn't mean being better than everyone else. I just wanted to compete against myself and see how far my abilities would take me. That's what truly excited me. And the truth was that I wasn't ready to give that up when it came to work.

Of course, with a bigger company and greater success, I had entered an entirely different arena with stiffer competition. Up until this point, MCP was providing cheese and other dairy products to other companies, which would sell them under their brand names. One of those companies was Olé Mexican Foods.

Like MCP, Olé had started as a small, family-owned business when its founder and president, Veronica Moreno, began selling tortillas in Atlanta, Georgia, in 1988 to meet the needs of a growing population of Mexican immigrants searching for the taste of home—as well as satisfying the growing desire of people born in the United States for Mexican food. She and her husband, Eduardo Moreno,

149

One Last Cheese

who served as her head of manufacturing, gradually began selling our queso fresco, as well as other Hispanic food products, under their company name.

This partnership worked well for us until I began having trouble with invoicing and payments. Whenever Olé delayed in paying me, of course it meant I had trouble meeting payments on my end for employee salaries and milk deliveries, and I didn't like it. Maybe because I'd grown up as the youngest son of an alcoholic father who never paid his bills on time, if it all, I had an aversion to being in debt.

"What we need to do," I said to Martina one night, as we were lying in bed after the kids were asleep and hashing through this particular problem, "is cut out the middleman. We're big enough now to have our own distribution centers. We could produce *queso* under our own name and sell it directly to customers without having to go through Olé or any other company."

"Do you really want to take that on?" Martina turned on her side to look at me. "You're hardly here as it is, Miguel. You're always *trabajando*. When is it going to be time for us to retire?"

"*Algun dia* soon," I promised. "But I'm still enjoying myself."

"Whatever," she grumbled and turned out her light.

Webster, it turned out, agreed with Martina. He kept pushing back whenever I suggested we should ramp up our cheese production even more. "I just don't want to work this hard anymore, Miguel," he said finally. "Remember that I'm older than you are, and I've been in this business a long time."

I sighed. "Then one of us is going to have to buy the other one out. We can't both be head of MCP, not if you want to slow down production and I want to increase it. What do you want to do?"

Ultimately, Webster sold me 40% of the company, and from then on we agreed that I'd be the one running the show and making key decisions about marketing, product development, and the future direction of the company. Webster would step back and just be our master cheesemaker, which was the part of the business he'd always loved.

During our partnership, I'd been hyper-focused on perfecting cheese recipes, getting our factory organized to run as efficiently as possible, and moving products out to the right customers. Now it was becoming increasingly clear to me that our growth would never reach its greatest potential unless we began distributing our own products. Companies like Olé Mexican Foods and Walmart had been buying our products and selling them under their own brand names, but using middlemen was eating up our profits—especially when these players dragged their feet in paying us.

Distributing our own products would be the only way to continue moving forward and growing the company. My singular goal was to place our products on shelves ourselves, with no middleman. To this end, we formed Latino Food Marketers, LLC.

Our next step was to find warehouses and hire employees around the country. It wasn't my intent to undercut the price Olé was putting on our cheese; I simply saw the size of the marketplace and realized there was plenty of room for both of us to sell cheese. Veronica and her husband had been doing business with us for many years by then, and I considered them friends. I had visited their factory and been to their house for dinner.

Once, when Veronica had called to say she needed more cheese from me, she said, "We're growing fast now, Miguel. Can you keep up?"

"Don't worry," I said. "Just tell me how many truckloads of cheese you need. I'll back you up."

Now that we'd formed Latino Food Marketers, I figured the Morenos would continue buying our cheese and selling it under their Olé label, while we sold the same cheeses under the name "La Chona," a name I'd picked because it's an area of Jalisco familiar to many immigrants and also slang for a woman who loves to dance. Their label had a Mexican flag, while ours had a cow jumping over a fence with a Mexican flag. Under the auspices of Latino Food Marketers, Martina and I opened distribution centers in Chicago, where we employed probably a hundred people, and in Atlanta and Denver.

Sadly, the Morenos didn't share our view that there was plenty of room in the marketplace for both of our brands. They wanted to control the market for Hispanic-style cheeses as well as tortillas and accused us of undercutting their prices. This wasn't true; if anything, my prices were higher than theirs. However, my marketing strategy was more aggressive in that I put more money into advertising and had our sales guys give away lots of free samples.

At one point, Olé had faxed me a contract saying Olé would buy exclusively from us, but I'd sent the contract back with changes and Veronica had never signed it. There was no legally binding agreement between us as a result.

I continued shipping products, and Olé continued paying for them—until our products reached Atlanta. Then they stopped paying us completely.

I called Veronica right away. "Hey, you need to pay for the cheese we shipped," I said, and she immediately began bitching about how our label was undercutting her sales. "That doesn't matter," I said, and pointed out that another competitor, Purple Crow tortillas, was already selling my cheese under his brand and didn't mind if I added my own label to the shelves. "There's room for everybody," I said.

"We have a contract, Miguel," she argued. "You're supposed to sell exclusively to us in this area."

"I made changes to the contract and sent it to you, but you never signed it, so we don't have any agreement of the sort." I was really getting angry at this point. "If you don't pay us for that cheese we sent you, we'll be in a fight. I'll sue your ass."

She didn't believe me and made noises about suing me. After we hung up, I told Fred to get a lawyer and sue Olé for the money they owed.

"It'll be expensive," Fred warned.

"I don't care. The one who hits first has a better chance of winning," I said, "and I'd rather start the fight here in Wisconsin than have to travel to Atlanta if she decides to sue us."

When the verdict was handed down, the judge agreed with us, too. Despite the fact that Olé had teamed up with Queso Margarita, a division of Quaker Oats (another company selling our cheese) to sue me for price undercutting, there was no evidence of that, and without any signed contract, we weren't bound to Olé in any way. The judge dismissed the charges against us. At the end of the lawsuit, Olé owed us more than a million dollars on its contract claim.

"I'm not finished with you yet, Miguel!" Veronica hissed as I left the courtroom. "You can't use the Mexican flag on your label. I'm going to sue you for that!"

"You can try, but you won't win," I said. "Nobody owns the Mexican flag."

But all of that courtroom drama paled in comparison to what happened to our company internally during that time: we discovered that Annette, Webster's wife, had turned against us. During the lawsuit with Olé, we realized that someone had been passing information to their lawyers through emails.

Why would Annette do such a thing? I had no idea. It was true that she had never liked Martina and me; she never thought we were good enough for her to even socialize with, never mind partner with, so maybe that was part of it. Or maybe she was angry because we'd bought most of Webster's shares in the company. In any case, once I hired a private investigator to tell us where the emails had originated, it was a straight forward matter for him to determine they were being created on Webster's computer.

One Last Cheese

That meant I had no choice: I had to fire Webster, my best friend, for betraying me during the lawsuit. I went to him and put it in plain terms. "Webster, your wife has been cheating behind my back," I said. "We have to divorce."

I sounded like a hard-ass, probably, but I was dying inside. Webster and I had been together since the beginning, and I still considered him my closest friend in the United States. I couldn't understand why he'd let his wife break us up like this. Even worse, I found out later that Webster hadn't known a thing about it. I'd blamed him for something he had no hand in, but it was too late. It was done. Webster and I were through forever.

■ ■ ■

Even though our queso fresco was so successful in the marketplace, I continued experimenting with the recipe, pushing myself to be better, always, even if it was only by 1%. This effort started when I was fighting that lawsuit against Olé. This was an extremely costly lawsuit, and I had to shell out the money for lawyers up front. Plus, Olé had stopped paying us for the cheese we'd sold them while the lawsuit was ongoing. That left us in a pinch financially.

The only way for us to make up for that shortfall would be to produce more cheese from the same amount of milk. Was that even possible?

I zeroed in on this goal and started tweaking the queso fresco recipe again, adding different quantities of vegetable oil. The queso fresco in Mexico all had vegetable oil in it; why shouldn't we put it in ours?

I started testing 100-pound batches of milk and vegetable oil in different quantities, cooked in small vats. The odd thing was that the cheese usually tasted absolutely perfect in those small batches, but when I tried producing it in 100,000-pound vats, the flavor changed.

I made quite a few errors during this time, like putting too much pressure on the homogenizer, which broke the cheese up completely, or adding vegetable oil when it was cold, which meant the fat in the vegetable oil hardened and didn't give me the texture I was looking for. Overall, I probably spent $700,000 trying to make the perfect, vegetable oil–infused queso fresco as I continued to experiment and threw every bad batch away.

Finally, I knew the recipe was just right. Originally, I'd made queso fresco with only whole milk, and my yield was about 12%. By adding vegetable oil to the recipe, now I not only had a much better, more Mexican flavor to the cheese, but yield jumped to 51%. That meant the cheese cost pennies to make, and the profit was tremendous. Even better, the taste was exactly right for our market, and sales boomed yet again.

■ ■ ■

Without Webster to hold me back from expanding the company even more, we grew 25% or 30% the next year and the next, too. We opened more distribution warehouses in other strategic locations nationwide to keep up with production and sales. Martina oversaw the warehouses, we'd hired an accountant, and I was mainly dealing with sales, focusing on getting the right person in each distribution center to target new customers and keep the old ones happy. In this business, as in most, customer satisfaction meant everything.

More companies approached, hoping to buy us out, but I was reveling in the heady feeling of having nobody controlling me. Besides, I'd come up with a new idea: I wanted to complete my line of Hispanic-style cheeses by producing cincho cheese. This was the natural outcome of my day-to-day practice of scouring the market to see what products were selling to our customers. Recently, I'd noticed cincho cheese popping up here and there in some of the smaller mom-and-pop stores that catered to immigrant communities. These stores were importing it from Mexico because nobody in the United States was making it. I could be the first.

Jose Gutierrez was still supporting our sales and took care of our routes and trucks through DQM, Distribudadora de Quesos Mexicanos. I decided to take him some cincho cheese that I'd bought at one of the stores. "Taste this and tell me if you think we could sell it in the United States," I said.

He chewed on a piece and grinned. "Miguel, if you can make this *queso*, I can sell tons of it."

Jose had brought his sister, Cynthia, up from Mexico, and we hired her to work as our finance operations manager in our Chicago warehouse, where she was in charge of invoices, payments, and documenting truck deliveries. She was a bubbly, short-haired, attractive young woman who did a good job. When she heard I was interested in cincho cheese, she suggested that I contact an acquaintance of hers, Jose Zurita, in Villahermosa.

"He's been bringing up cincho *queso* from Mexico to sell here," she said. She helped put me in touch with him, and before long Jose and I had a plan to meet in Mexico.

Cincho cheese originated in the state of Guerrero in southwestern Mexico, just south of Michoacan and Morelos. It's made from raw, semi-skimmed cow's milk, rennet, and salt. That's it. No preservatives at all. The cheese is so named because "cincho" means "belt" in English; when it's made in small batches by hand in Mexico, it's wrapped in a rope and left to sit, giving the cheese it's unique contouring around the rim. In Mexico, the cheese rind is often reddish in color from seasoning. The cheese itself is white or pale yellow.

My first step in adding cincho cheese to my line had to be finding the perfect recipe. Nobody else was making cincho cheese in the United States, and I was determined to be the first person to do that. Even more importantly, I wanted to identify and recreate the bacterial

The House that Cheese Built

culture for cincho cheese so I could bottle it or can it and sell the culture to other cheesemakers. Patenting and selling frozen culture starters of bacteria for a unique cheese would really set me apart from other cheesemakers in the United States—and would be hugely profitable.

I arranged for Martina and me to fly down to Mexico. My intent was to bring her to Villahermosa in Guerrero with me. I valued her input whenever I was considering a new business deal, and I loved traveling with her to new places. Martina was well organized, outgoing, and always ready for adventure.

To my surprise, though, once we were on the plane, Martina turned to me and said, "Miguel, *porfavor* don't be mad, but I think I'm going to let you do this cheese tasting thing alone, okay? I really want to go to my high school reunion this weekend. I'll just stay with my parents while you fly down to Villahermosa."

"What? Why? I thought we were going to have a fun weekend together. I was really looking forward to it."

She rolled her eyes at me. "You know as well as I do that you're taking this trip to check out *queso* factories. I get enough talk about cheese in the office. You go ahead. I want to go see my *amigos*. It's been a long time since we've gotten together."

I wanted to keep arguing, to persuade her to come with me, but when I saw how Martina's face lit up when she talked about the reunion, I realized she'd be really disappointed if she missed it. What could I do but accept her decision?

I flew down to Villahermosa alone. It was in the state of Tabasco, even farther south than Guerrero. Jose Zurita met me at the airport, holding up a sign so I'd recognize him. He was an amiable guy and seemed to have a good head on his shoulders. He'd been exporting the cincho cheese in small batches under his own label, he explained.

"Okay," I said, once we were in the car, "let's go see your factory."

Jose looked surprised. "Well, there's more than one factory, Miguel." He explained that, though he'd been exporting it under a single label, Hot Peppers, Inc., in reality the cheese was from several different factories.

"I'm not sure I like that idea," I said. "I like to keep my quality consistent, and of course I want the cheese to be safe." I knew the cincho cheese was made with raw milk and had to sit with a salted rind for at least 60 days; this was not only to bring out the flavor, but to ensure it was free of bacteria and safe to eat. Cincho was packaged when it was produced, but it couldn't be wrapped tightly or it wouldn't dry and age properly. "How can you guarantee that you'll be selling me the same product every time?"

"Don't worry about any of that, Miguel," Jose said quickly. "I haven't had any problems. Anyway, you don't have to take my word for it. The FDA inspectors always look at the cheese at the border. If they don't approve it, then I can't sell it to you, right?"

This was true. There was very little risk to me. If Jose brought the cheese to the border and the inspectors didn't let it pass through, then I wouldn't pay him for the shipment. It was as simple as that. We shook hands on the deal—I'd buy two pallets of the cheese, which came in 60-pound wheels—and Jose would be responsible for getting it across the border.

I went away excited and satisfied with our arrangement. If I imported the cincho cheese for now, I could get started on creating a laboratory culture while testing the US market to see if it was worth the investment. I saw this as a win-win.

Martina was supposed to meet me at the airport when I flew back, but she wasn't there when I arrived. I called her from the curb outside the airport. "*Estoy* here. Are you on your way?"

"Just about to leave. *Lo siento*. I lost track of time." She sounded breathless.

"Where are you?"

"With my *padre*."

"Okay, never mind," I said. "I'll take a taxi and meet you at the *rancho*."

It wasn't the homecoming I'd envisioned, but I had no reason to be suspicious.

We spent a few days with Martina's parents on the farm. It was relaxing enough, taking walks around the property and visiting, and I didn't want to ruin Martina's good time by talking about the deal I'd made with Jose. Truthfully, though, I spent a good part of the time in my own head, mulling over the business. Most of my friends had left Irapuato, and many of those who were still there just wanted to drink themselves blind. That wasn't for me. It occurred to me once again that I was as much at home in the United States as I was here, but neither place was wholly my country.

At the same time, I didn't feel at home anywhere, anymore, with Martina. Something had shifted between us. From the start of our relationship, she and I had been best friends, supporting each other through good times and bad. Martina had never wavered in her devotion to me, even back when her family tried to keep us apart and I seemed to have so few career prospects. She'd been ready to take on any challenge with me by her side: living on relative poverty, having children, moving to Mexico and back to the United States again, working with the Amish, and starting and growing a business.

My own devotion to her had been equally steady. Since the day we first met at the shooting range when I was 17 and she was 15, there had never been another woman in my life whom I'd cherished, respected, and desired the way I did Martina. My love for her, and my desire to build a family and a future with her, had propelled almost every decision I'd ever made. She was still my heart, my soul, my everything.

So what was wrong? It was tough to pinpoint, but I began noticing little things, like how we didn't stay up talking late into the night the way we once did, and how we'd stopped touching each other all of the time. We used to always hold hands and take showers together, but now she pulled away, even making up excuses not to make love with me.

Martina seemed to have lost interest in the house, too. There was never any food in the refrigerator or dinner waiting for me, and we rarely went away for weekends anymore. I couldn't figure out what was going on, but I missed her.

Should I have wooed her again, brought her flowers and made other grand romantic gestures? Most likely I was in the wrong for not doing that, but I was out straight, too busy running the company to do anything more than hope this was a phase in our relationship, and Martina would return to me.

■ ■ ■

Two things rapidly became clear to me when I returned from that trip to meet Jose Zurita. The first was this: if I could get my hands on the cincho cheese and develop a reliable culture to make it in the United States, it would be such a profitable venture that I could give up cheese making altogether.

The second thing that became obvious was that Martina was done with MCP. She wanted out. And as it happened, a buyer appeared at just the right time.

Not long after my meeting with Jose, I was approached again by Sigma Alimentos. Other companies had continued wooing us with buy-out offers; most recently it was another Mexican company, Lala foods. Sigma had been a customer of ours for a while and had made me an offer two years before, but at that time I wasn't ready to consider selling.

Since then, we'd made another jump in growth, from using a million to two million pounds of milk. More importantly, my profit margins were larger than those of most cheesemakers because I'd hit on exactly the right recipes for Hispanic-style cheeses, and I had orchestrated our factory equipment to run so efficiently that we only needed a minimal labor force.

Sigma is a Mexico-based global force in the world of food production. At the time they approached me, they had about 25 cheese factories. Today, the company is in 18 different countries and produced 1.8 million pounds of food in 2020. In addition to buying MCP and the recipes I'd developed, they were keen on having me stay on as a consultant for Grupo Alpha, the group that managed their cheese production in factories around the world. They had been impressed—even a bit astounded—when they toured my factory in Wisconsin and saw that we could produce the same amount of cheese with 106 employees that they were making in factories with 3,000 people or more.

"We need you to teach us to become more efficient, Miguel," they said and offered to fly me to Monterrey, Mexico, to meet with their group.

The meeting was smooth and productive. Martina came with me, and we were both impressed by the presentation Sigma gave and by their company facilities. Their management team seemed smart without being arrogant, and they made it clear they were impressed by how far we'd taken MCP. Best of all, the person leading the charge to acquire our company was a friendly, even-tempered guy named Mario. He was president of Sigma Alimentos and made it clear that they were interested in having me stay on as a consultant. This would be a chance for me to keep growing within an even larger family.

"The MCP acquisition reinforces our growth strategy in our target market, in which cheese plays a relevant role," said Mario, who explained that they planned to increase MCP's presence in the regions we presently served. They also hoped to gain additional market coverage by leveraging Sigma's distribution network and global business relationships. "This will be great for all of us."

161

One Last Cheese

We shook hands all around and agreed to do our due diligence to come up with numbers that would work for both sides.

"What do you think?" I asked Martina when we were on the flight home. "This could be really exciting. Something different for me, traveling around to analyze their production processes worldwide. And they'll pay me well as their consultant."

"I think you should jump at the chance," Martina said. "I know you're not ready to retire. And they have deep pockets. They'll make us a good offer. Better than anyone else's."

Of course, what I didn't know yet was that Martina had her own plans for the future.

■ ■ ■

Despite the heady ongoing negotiations to sell the company, I was still focused on the day-to-day management of MCP. I was especially keen on racing against the clock to develop that culture for cincho cheese I'd been hoping to produce before anyone else did that. We'd bought the first couple of pallets of cincho cheese from Jose Zurita after it was inspected by the FDA at the border crossing and released without any issues.

For the first time, we were selling an imported product. Our customers seemed to love the cincho, and I was excited about the market potential. I was also busy with the lab at the University of Wisconsin, trying to see if we could develop the culture.

We received our next, larger shipment of cincho cheese from Jose some months later. This time, though, we had some problems with customers returning the cheese because the rind still had moisture in it and the cheese had gone soft. I was worried that the speed of our sales might have caused Jose to hurry his production factories along so the cincho cheese hadn't had time enough to age. I decided to call him.

"People are complaining about the cincho cheese being soft," I said. "Did you change the recipe and the quality to improve the yield? Because, if you did, that's going to cause me *problemas*. I don't want recalls."

"No, man, it's all good," Jose assured me. "The inspectors wouldn't let it cross the border if it wasn't, right? That was just one bad batch."

"All right. Just don't let it happen again. And listen, you need to give me discounts and fix this problem. Otherwise I'm not going to pay you for the *queso*."

"Sure, Miguel, *no problema*," Jose said.

I had no reason not to trust him. After all, I'd discovered by now that focusing on a single goal at a time was the surest way to achieve it.

Looking back now, though, I wish I'd been less trusting of Jose. We hadn't known each other that long, and I'd already had problems with the quality of his product. The reality, though, is that you can, and will, make mistakes as you grow your business. When you end up having to pay for that mistake, as I would, in ways I never would have imagined possible, all you can do is remind yourself that mistakes and failures are also valuable lessons about how to do things differently in the future.

Part IV

BETRAYAL AND GRACE

Chapter 10

Big Money

The Recipe for Knowing When to Let Go.

A few months later, Cynthia called me to say there was a new problem with the cincho cheese: some of the cheese had been returned by our customers because it was moldy. I told her not to worry. "It's an easy fix," I said. "Tell the men at the warehouse to wash the outside of the *queso* with Devilcide. We'll let it dry out, then we can repackage it and sell it."

This was a common practice among cheesemakers. While fresh cheeses like ricotta should be thrown out if they're moldy—the mold can easily penetrate the cheese and might contaminate more than you see—mold doesn't penetrate far into hard cheeses like cheddar, Parmesan, cotija, or cincho. If you had a small piece of cheese at home, you would cut off the moldy part and eat the rest of it.

In fact, many cheeses are deliberately made with mold to add flavor or to help them grow a protective rind. Other cheeses, like blue cheese, are spiked with stainless steel rods to infuse mold deep into the cheese. There are also "washed-rind" cheeses where the cheesemakers rub solutions of carefully selected bacteria onto young cheeses during the aging process.

Some weeks later, I was visiting family in Mexico with Martina when I received another panicked phone call from Cynthia. "Miguel, there's a *problema*," she said, her voice high and tight with tension. "There are government inspectors all over the warehouse looking for

167

the last shipment of cincho *queso*, but it's not here. They're saying it's bad, and we need to recall it. Did you sell it?"

"*Claro* I sold it," I said. "Tell me why I shouldn't have. The signed release arrived from the inspectors at the border, right?"

"*Si*," she said, but her voice was shaking.

"All right, then everything is correct and in order. Tell the inspectors the truth. Do not lie to them. Say the FDA inspectors at the border signed the release, so I sold the *queso*. I didn't have any instructions to hold it."

"All right. So do I still have to recall the *queso?*"

"*Si*," I said. "You have to do exactly what the inspectors tell you to do, okay? And tell them I'm coming home and can meet them if they need me to do that. Meanwhile, tell your *hermano* that we need to recall any of that cheese we sold. We'll have to track it down."

"He's already on it," Cynthia said. "What else can I do?"

"Just be honest with the inspectors," I repeated. "Tell them we've sold the cheese because they released it, but we'll recall it as quickly as possible. We'll give the customers back their *dinero*. You don't have anything to worry about. Has anybody reported getting ill from eating our queso?"

"No, I don't think so," Cynthia said.

"Good."

"*¿Que pasa?* What's wrong?" Martina asked after I'd hung up, still swearing.

"The FDA inspectors are at the warehouse. They're saying we have to recall Jose Zurita's cincho."

She sighed and closed her eyes. "I told you not to mess around with that imported *queso*."

I took her hand and brought it to my lips for a kiss. "It'll be fine, *mi amor*. We've always complied with the FDA. At most we'll have to pay a fine."

I honestly believed that. All my life, I'd prided myself on being hard working, honest, and reliable. Surely the government would be on my side.

■ ■ ■

Back in Chicago, I went straight to the warehouse to ensure that every piece of cincho cheese we'd sold had been removed from the stores. None of my customers complained about this, since I returned their money immediately, but I visited every store to be completely sure that not one piece of my cincho cheese was still on the shelves.

I looked at the release Cynthia had received for the cheese, called a "bill of lading," and sure enough, there was a signature on the form from an FDA agent at the border. What the hell was going on? The inspector I'd met in the warehouse in Chicago seemed satisfied with our actions, but I still wanted to know the truth.

Naturally, one of the first people I called was Jose Zurita. "Why the hell did you sell me contaminated *queso*?" I shouted. "Look, you've got to come back here and help me fix this problem."

He played dumb, of course. "The cheese was fine when I sent it to the border," he said.

I hung up in frustration. Not long after that I received an email from Cynthia, saying the inspectors were going to come looking for the cincho cheese in our warehouses, but 311 boxes were still missing.

"Where are they?" I asked.

"New York," Cynthia said. "We sold it all so long ago that there's no chance we can recall it. What should we do?" She sounded panicked.

"Let me talk to Jose." I hung up and called him next.

When I explained the problem, Jose said, "So we'll just substitute the missing boxes with different boxes of *queso*. It'll be easy."

"Not a chance," I said. "If the *inspectores* come to the plant, they'll figure it out."

I knew from firsthand experience how one batch of cheese can differ from another, even in situations where I kept a tight rein on quality control. Jose's cincho *queso* was imported from different factories. It would be impossible for us to substitute identical cheese even if I'd wanted to be deceitful.

"I'm not going to lie to the *inspectores*," I said. "This is my reputation on the line. If they come to the warehouse, we'll just have to tell the truth."

Was I worried? Somewhat. But I had no idea just how worried I should be. Little did I know that it would take me more than four years, over a million dollars in attorney fees, and a manufactured guilty plea before my ordeal would be over—even though the FDA never went to my plant in Darlington to look for the cincho cheese. They only met with Cynthia and her boyfriend, Tony Zurita.

After that day, Jose refused to take my calls. He'd clearly washed his hands of the problem. I was pissed off but had no place to channel my rage. All I could do was hope this would blow over and not interfere with the reputation of Mexican Cheese Producers, which I'd worked so hard to create, or, more immediately, with the sale of our company to Sigma. Negotiations for the sale were now officially in motion.

■ ■ ■

Once the lawyers on both sides were satisfied with the valuation of Mexican Cheese Producers, Martina and I drove to Chicago to sign the papers finalizing the sale to Sigma. We'd agreed to split the profit 50–50, as equal partners. We'd also agreed to keep the cincho cheese out of the sale because of the recent problems with the FDA. Sigma bought the factory and all of my other cheese recipes, and I was instructed to send them a customer list so they'd have access to my buyers.

Being paid tens of millions of dollars was a surreal process, like something out of a James Bond movie: a guy from Switzerland called to tell me the money was being wired into our accounts even before we'd finished signing all of the papers with the lawyers. In a matter of seconds, Martina and I were wealthier than our wildest imaginings.

I don't think I've ever been happier or prouder of us than I was at that moment. My wife and I had worked tirelessly for three decades to sustain ourselves, raise our children, and build a company from the ground up that provided employment to hundreds of people and new food products to the marketplace. Now that we had the money and freedom to do as we wished, I was looking forward to many more adventures together.

Martina and I went out to dinner after the sale was finished and spent the night in Chicago. They were filming the movie *Batman Begins* downtown, and we had fun wandering the streets, watching the crew manage the lights and sets, on our way back to the hotel.

As we drove home the next morning, we talked about how strange it felt not to have anything to do. Every work responsibility had been lifted from our shoulders. There were no more deadlines to meet, no emergencies to attend, no employee hassles to sort, or equipment to fix.

"We're totally free now, Miguel!" she said. "Isn't it wonderful?"

"Yes," I said, though I was acutely aware of a hollow, lost feeling. The truth was that I didn't know what to do with my sudden freedom.

We celebrated the sale in style at home over dinner with the kids, accompanied by the most expensive champagne we could find at our local liquor store. The children were too young—13 and 16— to react much when we told them about the sale, other than to be happy that we were happy, I suppose.

"We'll have more time together as a family," I told them, "and your mother and I will set aside some money for you in a trust so you'll never have to worry about paying for college, or even buying a house."

"That's great, Dad," Tuti said, but I could tell her attention was elsewhere, probably on whatever was going on with her friends at school.

After dinner, Martina and I brought a second bottle of champagne outside, to drink by the bonfire pit in our back yard. We grew increasingly tipsy as the sparks flew into the velvety blackness overhead.

When at last we went inside to shower and undress, I was looking forward to the real celebration: making love with my wife, whom I desired every bit as much now, after three decades of marriage, as I had when we were teenagers. But Martina shook her head when I tried to embrace her and pulled away from me.

"I've had too much to drink, Miguel. *Lo siento*," she said. "I'm feeling really sick."

"That's fine," I said, though of course I was disappointed. She'd been pulling away more and more lately, and I missed our lovemaking.

Martina stood up, swaying a little, wobbly on her feet. "I need to tell you something, Miguel. Something *importante*."

"Hush." I put my finger to her lips. "Don't ever tell me something when you're drunk. You don't know what you're saying. Tell me in the morning, okay?"

"Okay," she mumbled, and hurried into the bathroom.

The next morning, we were nursing hangovers over coffee in the kitchen when I asked what she'd wanted to tell me the night before. "You were going to say something to me, Martina. What was it?"

She shook her head and laughed. "No idea," she said. "I forget what it was. I guess it must not have been very *importante*."

"All right. Tell me if you remember," I said.

With nothing else but a string of empty hours ahead of me that day, I went downstairs and began cleaning my guns. As I polished each rifle, I was overcome by regret and began to cry. What if selling the company had been the wrong decision? Mexican Cheese

Producers was where I'd found myself and grown as a cheesemaker, builder, marketer, and manager. Work had always provided me with inspiration, solace, and satisfaction. It had been the one thing in my life besides my family that I was proud of bringing into the world. Now it almost felt like I'd sold one of my children.

I'm lost without my company, I thought. *What am I going to do now?*

You're going to work for Sigma, I reminded myself. I would find new ways to grow professionally, and I was going to enjoy more time with my family. Life had given me this amazing second chance to embrace time with my wife and children. I vowed to make the most of that.

■ ■ ■

Not long after that, Cristobal and I went to a state shooting match. We both scored well during the match, but when he said he was tired, I agreed to drive home rather than wait around for the results to be announced.

I was always glad to have time alone with my son. I often missed the old days, when he was a little boy and I'd take him in my truck to work as I delivered cheese. In the past few months, between trying to negotiate the sale of our company, working with the University of Wisconsin laboratory on developing a bacterial culture for cincho cheese, and overseeing factory operations at Mexican Cheese Producers, I'd been right out straight. I couldn't remember the last time I'd seen my son for more than a few minutes.

Cristobal was 16, taller than I was, seemingly happy at school or when he was out with his friends, but sometimes withdrawn at home. Shooting used to give him joy, and that made me happy because he'd never had much passion for anything else. He was an average student and hadn't ever been an athletic star. In shooting competitions, though, wherever we went, Cristobal ended up in the finals. He was becoming so well known that practically every time I turned around at a competition, someone would ask, "Hey, are you Cristobal's dad?" I was always so proud to say yes.

Lately, though, I'd noticed that his interest in shooting was flagging. He was reluctant to practice, and that day I asked him why. He gave me that typical teen shrug.

"Come on. Talk to me," I said. "Look, you have real talent at this. It's in your blood to be a champion. You could make it as far as the Olympics. What's holding you back?"

"I don't know, Dad," he said. "I like shooting, but I like my friends, and I want to see them more. There's this girl, too."

"There's always going to be a girl," I said, frustrated that he'd just throw away his future like that. At the same time, I could hardly give him relationship advice. Hadn't I done exactly the same thing at his age? Met a girl and fallen hopelessly in love?

At least with me it had turned out all right. Maybe it would for him, too. I hoped so.

We'd been driving for about three hours when we got a phone call in the car from the shooting range. "Where are you and your son?" asked the guy managing the competition. "The two of you are tied for first place. You need to come back here and have a shoot-off!"

I told him we were too far away to turn around now, and that we'd arrange to come back for the shoot-off another day. I hung up and told Cristobal, and we burst out laughing. "You know what, kid, I want to beat you," I said.

"Yeah, but I won't let you," he said.

"We'll see," I said, happy that he was at least still willing to try.

■ ■ ■

Shortly after that shooting match, Sigma asked me to tour a factory in Peru in my new role as director of their cheese industry. When I arrived at the small airport in Monroe, I found a private jet idling on the runway, gleaming and shark-nosed. Men in fine suits—all of them directors with Sigma Alimentos—greeted me with enthusiastic handshakes. "Mr. Leal, welcome! Glad to have you with us today."

Inside, the jet looked just like the ones I'd seen in James Bond films, with comfortable, roomy seats for a dozen people, and our own flight attendant to bring us whatever we needed. Martina had driven me to the airport, and as the ground receded rapidly beneath me, I waved, despite knowing there was no chance she could see me. Once again, I had that image of myself as lost, like a castaway in a foreign land. It seemed very wrong to be doing this without my wife at my side. She'd always been my best, most trusted partner.

In Peru, Sigma wanted to acquire a factory that produced both meat and cheese products. My primary task was to inspect the vats and pipelines to make certain there were no holes or other avenues for contamination. I gave the Sigma executives the green light, and they assured me that I'd be in charge of retrofitting the equipment once they purchased the company.

Sigma sent me all over Latin America over the next few years. They'd given me a salaried position with bonuses, so I was receiving a hefty paycheck of anywhere from $600,000 to $800,000 annually for doing work I loved. My job was to visit each of their factories— the ones Sigma already owned and the ones they were thinking of acquiring—and make a plan to help them decide on next steps to improve the quality of their cheese and decrease production costs.

In most instances, I would easily spot the flaws in equipment design or setup and offer a plan for changing over to more updated equipment, cleaner practices, or a completely different flow of operations. Over time, I helped Sigma save millions of dollars a year by improving their efficiency and yield.

Their most urgent need for help was in Mexico, where they owned eight factories, all of which had problems. I analyzed the production processes at each and made recommendations. Some

175

Big Money

factories were doomed to close. There were too many problems, typically with sanitation or old and rusty equipment, for us to successfully rehabilitate them. In others, I was able to turn them around, putting in equipment and production practices similar to what I'd been using at my factory in Wisconsin.

Sometimes the whole process of rehabbing a factory in Mexico started with changing the sewer system. Or in one case, I saw that they were keeping the milk in open vats, as the Amish had done. The workers here had to jump inside these 20,000-pound vats of milk during the cheese-making process, which of course meant they were contaminating it. This was potentially treacherous in Mexico's hot, humid weather, where milk spoiled so easily and bacterial cultures thrived. We took away the open vats and set up a system where the milk was kept cold and in closed containers. We also automated the process so the cheese could be made more efficiently and more safely.

A second factory in Mexico, this time in Jalisco, had a maggot problem because milk was leaking into the tanks. A lot of whey was being washed down the drains and making its way into the sewer pipes. We managed to save that one, too, but it required first moving all of the production to one of the other factories, then closing this one down so we could install all new equipment and pipes.

In 2010, Sigma asked me to travel to the Dominican Republic to overhaul a cheese factory there. We spent most of the day in a meeting after I'd completed the initial tour of the factory, analyzing how to change the logistics of how the pipes were laid in the factory. Just as we were returning to our hotel that afternoon, there was an earthquake. We had to race up to the top of the highest mountain and stay with some other Sigma engineers because our hotel was on the ocean and everyone was worried about a tsunami.

The epicenter of the 7.2-magnitude earthquake was in neighboring Haiti. The experience brought back terrible memories of searching for my father's body long ago, but I stayed long enough to help Sigma ship food from their Dominican factory to Haiti, where people were starving and scrambling for shelter.

Despite my fear of being caught in an earthquake, I loved every minute of the work I did for Sigma. It felt like I was in the right place at the right time. I was completely in my element because the job required me to be a creative problem solver. The best part about consulting was the new rhythms in my life. I had numerous opportunities to travel to new countries and try to make their factories cleaner, more efficient, and more productive—all arranged according to my own schedule. I began fantasizing about having actual weekends and vacations.

Maybe we'll buy an RV, I thought, *and take a coast-to-coast road trip over the summer.* After all, Tuti was 14, and Cristobal was nearly 17. They wouldn't be with us much longer. It was time for me to slow down the pace of my life enough so I could treasure these last years with my children before they left home and launched into their own adult lives.

And then what? Then Martina and I would be alone again at last. I hoped she'd be happier then. She continued to remain distracted, or even absent, at home, and I could tell that she was frustrated, seeing how happy and productive I was, while she had so little to do. She began flying back and forth to Mexico to oversee our car wash business, and complained about my brother Carlos. We'd given him the job of managing the car wash, and Martina was convinced he was stealing money; she also thought we were paying him too much, even though Carlos was making only 40,000 pesos a month—a paltry amount.

"The whole point of having the car wash was to help our *familias*," I pointed out.

"Still, that doesn't mean we should let your *hermano* steal from us. I'm going to *México* to straighten things out," Martina declared.

177

Big Money

I put my hands up in surrender. "*Esta bien*, do what you need to do," I said, because I was too busy with Sigma to really pay much attention to what Martina was up to in Mexico. She'd never been very creative—all of the ideas for our business had been mine—but she was well-organized and good with numbers. I trusted her to do the right thing.

That was another key mistake.

■ ■ ■

Truthfully, I had mostly forgotten about the FDA investigation because I'd been so busy with Sigma over the past few years. Then one day I received a call from one of the FDA agents, Ron Melham. "Mr. Leal?" he said.

"Yes?"

"I'm calling to inform you that the FDA is opening an official case against Mexican Cheese Producers. We're investigating your sale of contaminated cheese."

"What do you mean?" My heart was racing and my mouth went bone dry. "I did everything by the book. I cooperated with the inspectors and picked up all of the cheese from the customers. Nobody has gotten sick from my cheese!"

"Well, let's hope nobody does get sick," he said, "or you'll have to go to jail."

"But that cheese isn't even mine!" I yelled, really pissed off now. How could they accuse me of selling contaminated cheese when this wasn't a product I'd made and the cheese had been cleared by customs when it crossed the border?

We hung up soon after that. My hands were shaking, I was so angry. *This whole thing is ridiculous*, I told myself.

■ ■ ■

With the influx of immigrants working on dairy farms and in factories like ours, and with the arrival of Latinx-owned businesses like the new Mexican restaurant in town, the anti-immigrant sentiment had started to rear its ugly head in town.

I experienced this firsthand one ordinary weekday afternoon. By the time Webster and I had built our second factory to accommodate our continuing increase in sales, I'd rented an office above a bank in downtown Monroe to accommodate our growing staff and volume of paperwork. Martina could no longer keep up with the invoices, payroll, and taxes alone, so I'd hired Fred Yoder to act as our chief financial officer. I'd met Fred when he was chief executive officer of Wisconsin Cheese Group because I'd always admired his gruff honesty. He was a short, balding man who'd always tell you the truth about your finances and what you needed to do to keep on the right side of the IRS, and I admired that about him.

One day, I stopped in the bank downstairs to wire money to Martina, who was visiting her family in Irapuato and in the process of buying a car wash. We'd heard it was for sale through my brother Pedro and knew it was a good business opportunity; if nothing else, we could keep family members employed. I couldn't get away, so Martina had flown down to Mexico to finalize the sale.

I was just about to close my computer and find some lunch when my daughter called. "Hey, Dad, how about if I pick you up, and we can have lunch together?" she said.

"Sure." I was delighted. I had often spent time alone with Cristobal, since we traveled to shooting competitions together, but it was harder to find those special one-on-one moments with Tuti.

As I exited the building to meet her at the corner, I received a phone call and began talking to the person on the other end while I glanced into the bank. It was completely empty. That was strange; I'd never seen the bank empty during business hours.

When I opened the heavily-tinted double doors leading out of the building, I was still on the phone; I stopped short when I was surrounded by at least 50 police officers outside, all pointing guns at me.

"Freeze!" one of the officers yelled at me. "Put your phone down, and lie on the ground!"

I complied, and was shocked when they handcuffed me and hauled me to my feet. "What the fuck is this?" I asked. "Why are you arresting me?" My heart was pounding so hard it felt like my ribs might crack from the pressure. Of course my first thought was that this must have something to do with the FDA investigation. A tiny, paranoid part of me wondered if they were just going to throw me in jail even before there was a trial.

"Just keep your mouth shut," one of the cops said. He began frisking me, searching in my pockets for a weapon. When he found the receipt for the $600,000 I'd wired to Martina, he started shouting again. "What's this? Whose fucking money did you steal, asshole?"

"That's *my* freakin' money, you dumb ass!" I said. "Go on inside. Ask the teller. I have an office upstairs, and I own a factory here in town. I come in every week. She *knows* me!" I was furious but terrified as well. The police officers were still pointing their guns directly at me. If this were Mexico, I'd probably be dead by now, no questions asked. All it takes is one trigger-happy cop.

By now, I'd overheard enough conversation among the police officers around me to know that the bank had been robbed by "one of those damn Mexicans" just before I'd come downstairs. One of the cops went into the bank now and came out again with the teller who had taken my deposit minutes earlier. To my horror, when he pointed to me, she shook her head.

"I don't know him," she said.

"Oh, come on," I said. "You know me. I'm here every day. I've been renting that office upstairs for two years!"

"Sorry," she mumbled, and turned away.

The police dragged me over to a corner, where another Mexican guy stood in handcuffs. In Spanish, he said, "Help me out, help me out!" to me.

"Fuck you," I said. "Get out of my face, you *pinche* thief!"

The police put me in the back of a police car—you don't know what it's like to be humiliated, until that happens to you in front of the whole town where you've been doing business—and drove me to the station, where they handcuffed me to a chair in one of their offices. There, they played a video from the security cameras, stopping the film when they saw me on it.

"See, that's you, going inside the bank building," they said. "Don't try to deny it!"

"Of course that's me," I said. "I already told you that I have an office upstairs. Where's the sheriff? I want to see the sheriff!"

The sheriff of Monroe had been to my house for dinner. When he appeared, he said, "Miguel, please. Just calm down. You're only making thing worse."

I was too pissed off to be calm. "You've known me for a long time, but you lock me up?" I accused. "It's because I'm Mexican, isn't it?"

"Please, Miguel," he said. "Please just be quiet."

"I'll be quiet when you take off these fucking handcuffs!" I said.

Eventually they examined my wallet, found my identification, and discovered I'd been telling the truth. They also told me that a man from Mexico had come into Mexican Cheese Producers, looking for work. He'd somehow gotten his hands on a paycheck and had made false ones to cash around town, even faking my signature on the checks.

"Go home, Miguel," the sheriff said wearily. "I'll see you soon."

Not if I can help it, I thought, and stormed out of the jail. Just when I'd started thinking I belonged here, I'd found ample proof that I was still a castaway in the United States.

■ ■ ■

I had been traveling for Sigma most of the month, but I happened to be at home, puttering around in the garage, when I received another phone call from the FDA agent, Ron Melham.

"Mr. Leal," he said, "I'm glad I caught you. I just wanted to give you a head's up and let you know that you're going to get served papers tomorrow by agents from the Department of Justice."

"What papers?" I asked in shock, stepping outside, onto the driveway, to gulp the fresh air so I wouldn't pass out. "What are you talking about?"

"You know full well what I'm talking about, Mr. Leal. You're being accused of conspiracy to distribute potentially harmful food products to the public. You could have poisoned a lot of people. We need to hold you accountable for that. Agents will meet you in the coffee shop near your office tomorrow to serve you official papers from the Department of Justice, letting you know that the investigation is official now. We expect your full cooperation."

"I don't understand," I sputtered. "What else can I do to make this go away? I've done everything right." The driveway seemed to sway beneath me.

"Just cooperate with us, please, Mr. Leal, and it will all go much better for you." He hung up.

My legs gave out beneath me, and I had to sit down on the driveway. How was this happening, after all of the hard work I'd put into the company and the sacrifices I'd made?

Eventually I gathered enough strength to go back inside, where I called frantically for Martina. She answered from the family room, where she was watching television; when I told her about the call, however, she looked unconcerned. "They don't have *nada* on you," she said. "Don't worry so much."

"Aren't you upset, though? This is all so unfair. I don't even understand the accusation, but the agents are on their way to my office tomorrow to serve me with papers! We need to resolve this problem."

She shrugged and turned her attention back to the TV. "I'm sorry you're going through this."

Her tone was so aloof that I froze, shell-shocked, and had to replay her comment in my head to make sure I'd heard her correctly. When I'd recovered, I said, "What do you mean, you're sorry *I'm* going through this? We're in this together!"

Martina shook her head. Her face was still oddly expressionless. "No, Miguel, this is your *problema*. We're not partners anymore, remember? Mexican Cheese Producers no longer exists as a company. And *you* bought cincho cheese from Jose Zurita, not me."

"I may have bought the *queso*, but you supervise Cynthia, and she received it in the warehouse," I said. "So why is this only my problem?"

She sighed. "*Mira*, don't worry. It will all be fine."

I left her, still feeling confused, but hoped she was right.

The agents showed up at the coffee shop by my office the next morning. They weren't in uniforms, just ordinary suits, but they wore guns in shoulder holsters beneath their jackets. It was clear from their crew cuts and muscular builds that they were ex-military men and meant business. They were polite, declining the coffee I offered to buy them, and served me the papers.

"Okay, buddy, you've been served," one of them said before they left. "You don't look like the kind of guy who has problems, but take our advice, Mr. Leal, and get yourself a lawyer. If you can't afford to defend yourself, the government will appoint a public defender in your name. Here's a card with the address of the Federal Building in Chicago. You can talk to the lawyers there."

Martina and I drove to the Federal Building in Chicago the next morning. My anger began building again on the way. How could the FDA sue me, when I'd done nothing wrong? Martina, on the other hand, appeared serene. She was freshly showered and in full makeup. Her hair was blown straight, and her legs looked toned and tanned beneath her short skirt. She'd been dressing this way, lately, more provocatively, and I couldn't help but say something about it in the car.

She glanced at me. "You want the lawyers to be on our side, right?" she said. "It won't hurt to have them think I'm attractive."

I swallowed hard. Maybe she really was trying to help me. God, I hoped so. I'd never needed Martina on my side more than at that moment.

The drive to Chicago was only an hour but felt like an eternity. When we arrived, I hesitated on the steps and looked up at the massive Federal Building, my fury in the car now replaced with the kind of fear that makes you feel cold all over. This building was designed to make people feel cold: 10 stories tall, flat-roofed, and made of brick and cement with little ornamental detail to soften its features. Only the entryway, with its Gothic details, relieved the stern looking exterior.

The public defender, Joseph, turned out to be a young, nervous-looking guy. He shook my hand too eagerly and invited us to sit down in his office and discuss the case.

"I'm not going to jail for this," I said at once.

"Let's hope not," Joseph said. "But the FDA is accusing you of conspiracy. That's a big problem. You definitely need to pay for an attorney to defend you." Probably he'd taken one look at my fine suit and shirt, and at Martina's expensive shoes and handbag, and decided that, unlike most of his clients, we could afford to pay for our own lawyer.

"How much will that cost?" Martina asked.

"Probably at least a $25,000 retainer up front."

"Twenty-five *thousand*?" I sputtered furiously. "How can this cost me that much money? That's too expensive!"

"Not if it keeps you out of jail," Joseph said.

"Jail?" My stomach knotted. "Am I really going to jail for this?"

"Let's hope not," Joseph said. "But like I said, it's going to cost you. Look, let's go upstairs and see the guy in charge of the investigation for the FDA. Maybe that'll help you decide what to do."

Martina waited downstairs while I took the elevator upstairs to the FDA offices with Joseph. "Whatever you do, Miguel, do not tell those guys how much *dinero* we got when we sold the company," she warned.

"Okay," I said, because when it came to money, I always listened to her.

I had met several FDA agents, but never Renato Mariotti, the director of the Chicago office. He was dark-haired with a chubby build and a long face. After Joseph introduced us, he said, "Miguel, do you know Jose Zurita?"

"Yes, of course," I said.

"Well, okay, so you guys are in a world of trouble," Renato said.

"Why me? I haven't done anything wrong. Jose sold me the cheese, and the inspectors signed the papers at the border. I don't understand any of this!"

We talked for a few minutes more, about Mexican Cheese Producers, Jose Zurita, the cincho cheese, and the fact that Martina and I had sold the company to Sigma without including the cincho cheese in the sale.

"Why not?" Renato asked with a smug look.

"Because we wanted to keep the recipe," I said, and shifted in my chair. I'd never been a good liar.

"No, it's because you knew what was going on, didn't you, Miguel?" Renato leaned toward me across his desk, breathing coffee into my face. "You knew that cheese was dirty when you brought it into this country! Those signatures on the paper at the border were falsified, as you well know. Your colleague Cynthia signed for that cheese. It was never approved at the border, and now you and Jose Zurita are going down for your mistake. I'm accusing you

185

Big Money

of conspiracy to poison the people of the United States with your cheese. You could get 19 years in jail for this."

Joseph stood up hastily. "Come on, Miguel. We're done here."

I followed him on shaking legs to the elevator, Renato dogging my heels. The elevator came at once, thank God, and we stepped into it. I was having trouble breathing and had to lean against the back wall of the elevator. That number was running through my head: *nineteen years, nineteen years in jail! Nineteen years!*

Renato called to me as the doors began to close. "I'm going to put you in jail for 20 years, Miguel!"

I almost passed out in the elevator. I was panting and clutching at my collar, trying to loosen it so I could breathe. *Why were they doing this to me?* I asked myself over and over. *Why?* Joseph kept a close eye on me but remained silent.

Downstairs, Martina was sipping a coffee. She gave me a sharp look. I must have looked like a man on death row who's too sick to eat his last supper. In the mirrored elevator walls, I'd seen my pasty complexion and pinched white lips. "What happened?" Martina asked. "What the fuck did you tell them, Miguel? You didn't tell them how much we sold the company for, did you? Because they're going to go after our *dinero* if you did."

"I did," I said weakly. "*Lo siento.*"

"You dumb *pinche idiota*!" she shrieked. "What the fuck is *wrong* with you?"

Everything, I wanted to say, but I had no voice at that moment. I felt as small and powerless as I used to feel whenever my father came after me in a rage. All I wanted to do was crawl into a corner and hide.

I started walking blindly out of the cafe. "*Vamonos.*"

Martina stood up and snapped her pocketbook strap over one shoulder. "Where to?"

"*Necesitamos* a better lawyer. Sorry, Joseph. You're fired. We're going to Katten right now."

Katten Muchin Rosenman, LLP, was the law firm that had handled the sale of our company to Sigma. Martina and Fred, our accountant, had worked closely with them to finalize the negotiations and sale of Mexican Cheese Producers. Katten's attorneys welcomed us like friends—as well they should, since we'd done an enormous business deal with them so recently.

I was still in shock, unnerved by my visit with Renato, but Martina seemed suddenly animated. Provocative, even: she crossed and uncrossed her legs, lifting her knees too high in her short skirt, and sat with her back arched and her chest pushed out. What the hell was she up to? She talked and talked, telling them what was going on and what had happened, and it was clear to all of us that she would be in charge of running this case.

"Martina, what's wrong with you? What were you doing in there?" I demanded when we left the office after plunking down a hefty retainer fee. Katten knew exactly how much money we had; they were charging us top dollar to have them defend us in this FDA case.

"I'm handling things," she said, "since it's obvious that you can't."

She was right. I felt out of my depth. I'd always trusted Martina and had never doubted her judgment. Since our marriage, I had given her full control over all of the most important decisions in my life: our finances, how to run our company, where to live and vacation, when to build a new house, how many children we would have and how to raise them, and when to sell the company we'd built together. I had never seen this as anything other than a healthy partnership.

It was only lately that I'd begun to doubt her loyalty, but now I pushed those doubts aside. If I couldn't trust Martina with my business, my heart, and my life, then who could I trust in this world?

187

Big Money

Probably there's no better evidence of how desperately anxious I felt about the impending court case than this: when Martina suggested that we see El Padrino, a Cuban witch doctor, to find out our fate, I agreed.

El Padrino saw his clients in the basement room of an ordinary looking suburban house. Here, he'd set up an altar with chairs around it, and the room was full of candles, flowers, chicken feathers, and crosses. "What is it you want to know?" he asked when I sat down with him.

I cut right to the chase. "Whether I'm going to jail for something I didn't do."

He nodded, lit some candles, closed his eyes, and started praying and singing. "You will not go to jail if you truly believe," he concluded and encouraged me to drop money into his jar. Not just a little money, either. With Martina encouraging me to "stop being so tight," I gave the guy $400. In exchange I received necklaces, candles, and some strange smelling potions to use at home, with instructions for follow-up visits. I went several more times to see El Padrino over the next six months, but each time I believed less, despite Martina's fervent assurances that this guy could keep me out of jail.

■ ■ ■

People often ask me about selling the company to Sigma. The recipe for knowing when to let go of your company is different for everyone. Entrepreneurs who start a new company often feel, as I did, that this is their "baby." When you own a business, you want to see it grow up, so you spend countless hours and extreme amounts of money in raising it to be a profitable venture. Often, you hold onto the business for too long, limiting its growth potential or eventually letting it die. If you don't know how to exit, you risk limiting your own potential.

The House that Cheese Built

There are three basic ingredients for knowing when to let go of a company. The first is the physical health barometer. Through the years, I had worked so many hours that I was in poor physical health; this is fairly typical of entrepreneurs and a clear sign that the business has either exceeded your capacity for running it at scale or you need more resources and a better team in place. If physical health is a problem, as it was for me, then it's time to let go.

A second ingredient is generational wealth. I had hoped that my children would want to take over my business, but neither showed any interest. If they had, I might have kept the business and continued growing our family's generational wealth.

Finally, the third ingredient is money: Do you have enough? When considering an exit, don't focus on a certain valuation. Instead, determine if the buyout offer will satisfy your financial needs and lifestyle. Otherwise, hold onto the business and let it keep growing.

I sold my company at the perfect time for me. It's just too bad everything else in my life fell apart at the same time. Then again, there are always lessons to learn in failure. I was about to discover more personal resources I didn't know I possessed. As bad as things got, eventually I was able to see my situation as an opportunity for growth.

Chapter 11

Betrayal

Humbling Failures Can Be Opportunities to Pay Attention and Start Again.

One of the hardest things I had to do after seeing Renato and realizing how serious this FDA case was against me was resign from Sigma. I flew down to Monterrey to meet with Sigma's president, Mario, and told him what was going on. "I'm worried I might have to go to jail," I said, "and I really need to devote all of my energy to fighting these accusations."

Mario walked me outside and shook my hand. "I hope everything goes well. If you do end up in jail, Miguel, don't worry. I'll come and see you."

"I don't want that," I said, horrified by the idea. "If I go to jail, I'll come see you when I get out."

I left then to take a cab back to the airport, shaking and crying hard. I'd been up on a cloud, at the height of my professional success and personal happiness with my family, and suddenly someone had pulled me off. I'd hit the ground so hard that I was sure I'd hit bottom, but I was wrong. There was lower, still, that I would have to fall.

■ ■ ■

As the lawyers at Katten continued to work with me on the case, charging me tens of thousands of dollars every month, the FDA agents were calling me and encouraging me to cooperate. When I told the lawyers this, they encouraged me to cooperate with the FDA. "You do whatever they ask you to do," they said, "and we can get the judge to reduce your sentence because you've been helping them."

This made sense to me. So when the FDA contacted me with a proposal, I listened: if I could help them nail Jose Zurita, who was wanted for various crimes and remained untouchable in Mexico, they could give me a decent plea bargain deal.

"Okay," I said, "tell me what you want me to do."

"Tell him you have a new chain of restaurants that wants to buy cincho cheese, and ask him to bring you half a truck," suggested one of the agents. "Encourage him to bring the cheese across the border. We can run a sting operation and capture him there."

I frowned. "That's not a lot of cheese. He already knows I'm angry because he sold me contaminated cheese. Would it be more tempting for him if I said I wanted two truckloads or something? Or if, I don't know, if you somehow set it up so Jose Zurita would think he'd won tickets for his family to Disney World? Wouldn't he be more likely to cross the border if there was a bigger reward that made the risk worthwhile? He knows you guys are after him."

"Just do it, Miguel," the agents said, "and things will go better for you.

Naturally, I was eager to help the agents nab Jose Zurita—he'd screwed me over, too—and I was willing to do anything to avoid jail time. So I flew down to Mexico—with the FDA's permission to leave the country, of course—and asked my friend Felipe, who had been helping me sell cheese in the New York area, to find Jose Zurita for me. Felipe did, and when I flew back to Chicago I gave Felipe's phone number to the lawyers.

"He's aware of what's going on," I said. "He's my friend and knows I'm innocent, so he's willing to help us by contacting Jose Zurita and setting things up for you. Or if you want, I'll fly down to

Mexico and bring you Jose myself. I'll get him in a car with me and you can arrest him across the border."

When my lawyers caught wind of this plan, however, they were horrified. "It's a bad idea for you to try to negotiate with the FDA, Miguel," they warned, and I was terrified all over again. What if I'd made a mistake, and the case against me would be stronger because I'd contacted Jose Zurita? I felt like wolves were biting my legs, tearing at the skin, but I couldn't get away.

In the end, the FDA never managed to trap Jose—he was too smart to show up at the Walmart where they'd arranged a meeting with him—and the attorneys at Katten continued to bleed me dry.

■ ■ ■

I had an appointment to get my fingerprints taken at the police station the week after the whole debacle with Jose Zurita. I was feeling nervous about the case and very alone, since Martina continued to be oddly removed from me, even in the bedroom. I needed my brother Pedro's company. He, of all my brothers, was as sensitive as I was, and I knew he'd be a great comfort.

"Fine," Martina said when I told her I'd bought Pedro a ticket. "That'll work out well. I'll go down to Mexico, visit my mom, and check on the business while Pedro's here."

Pedro and I had a wonderful time the first day he was here, talking late into the night over a few drinks. As the evening wound down, though, my brother began looking worried and said he needed to tell me something.

"You know what, Pedro, let's just go to sleep," I said. "We've had a great day, and I'm tired. You can talk to me in the morning after *los ninos* go to school, okay?"

He agreed, and I fell into a deep, dreamless sleep, anesthetized by alcohol and the comfort of my brother's presence.

The next morning, I made us some coffee and breakfast. I was bustling around the kitchen afterward, cleaning up, when Pedro said, "Miguel, sit down."

I turned around, surprised by his stern tone. When I saw the serious expression on my brother's face, I sat down across the table from him and folded my hands. "Okay. Tell me whatever it is you need to say."

Pedro took a deep breath and shuddered a little, clasping his hands around the coffee mug as if he had to hold himself firmly in place. "*Mira*, Miguel, we're not a hundred percent sure, but I think Martina's cheating on you."

I snorted. "No, come on. No way. Martina would never do that!"

"It's not just me who thinks this," Pedro said. "Alejandra thinks the same thing."

If our sister said it, I had to take this accusation more seriously. Alejandra had always been the most serious among us. "I don't believe you," I said stubbornly. "Who's *el hombre*?"

"Alejandro Monterrey," he said.

I sucked in my breath in shock. I knew that name: Alejandro was one of Martina's high school classmates. The pieces fell into place. Was that why Martina had insisted on going to her high school reunion instead of coming to Merida with me to see Jose Zurita? Was Alejandro the real reason she was flying down to Mexico so often, allegedly to check on the car wash business and visit her mom?

"*Chingado*. No way," I repeated, but this time my tone wasn't so sure.

"Look, we don't know for sure that it's true. Let me check on things for you in *México*, okay? Alejandra said she'd help us."

I nodded as Pedro explained that our sister was friends with Alejandro's ex-wife, so it would be easy enough for her to find out. Pedro then outlined an outrageous plan for communicating the information to me. He and I were partners on a farm where we grew green peppers. Martina and I had bought the farm as another business opportunity; it had a huge greenhouse and several acres, and Pedro managed it for us. Pedro suggested that he could go back to Mexico and ask our sister to spy on Martina, to see if she was actually visiting her mom or seeing her lover.

"She'll tell me the situation, and I'll call you when we know for sure," he said. "If I say the *chiles* are red, then it's for sure 100% that Martina's having an affair. If I say the *chiles* are green, then we made a mistake. And if I tell you the *chiles* are yellow, that means we don't know, okay?"

"Okay," I said, feeling sick to my stomach, reeling over the impossibility that the woman I had loved for more than three decades might not be who I thought she was.

Pedro stayed for a week. During that time I kept pestering him with questions about Martina and Alejandro, saying, "You have to be wrong. This can't be true," but believing that less and less as the days passed. I called Martina, too, not to ask her directly if she was having an affair, but to see if I could tell anything was wrong by the tone of her voice.

Martina sounded as she always did, serene and even upbeat. "I'm doing fine," she said. "I'm here in Irapuato. *Te amo*. I hope you're having lots of fun with Pedro."

"Oh, absolutely," I said, and hung up, my hands shaking because I no longer trusted her.

On May 12, I took Pedro to the airport and picked up Martina. We had an appointment at the police station to have my fingerprints taken. Martina kissed me at the airport and seemed the same as always, and I told myself that Pedro was delusional. Martina was here with me, and everything was fine. Now we just had to get through this FDA investigation, and once that was done, we could enjoy our retirement in style.

At the police station, though, my courage evaporated as I stood in line, waiting for my fingerprints to be taken. Cynthia Gutierrez was there, too, among the dozens of people waiting to be fingerprinted. I felt my fury rise at the sight of her bowed head. Our lawyers had sent an investigator out to determine what had really happened with the cincho cheese.

The truth was this: Cynthia Guttierez, who was supposedly being supervised by Martina at the warehouse, knew that there had to be a release form from the FDA before she paid for the deliveries of cincho cheese. The first delivery a year ago had gone off without a hitch; we'd started with half a truck of cincho cheese and had sold it all without any problems with the customers. The next time we ordered cheese, we asked for three semi-loads. Apparently the FDA had put a hold on those trucks at the border, but Cynthia was dating Jose Zurita's brother, Tony. It was Tony who had convinced Cynthia to falsify the papers, which was why I didn't know there had been a hold put on the cheese. I wanted to shout at her when I saw her in line for fingerprinting, to ask how she could have been so stupid, but we'd been forbidden by our attorneys to speak with one another. I passed by without even a glance in her direction.

As I approached the room where they'd take my fingerprints, a tall Black man was brought in by the police. He was handcuffed, his arms and neck were heavily tattooed, and his chest and thighs and arms bulged with muscles in places I didn't even know you could have muscles. When the police tried to take his photograph, he fought them until several men held him down. They looped a chain around his ankles then to subdue him. He was so terrifying that I nearly puked on the spot, imagining having to be locked up with guys like that for 19 years and pointlessly converting that to a sentence of an even more daunting 228 months.

I held it together while they fingerprinted me and told me to strip so they could check for tattoos. The police looked through my wallet to see if I had any drugs or other contraband. Finally an officer asked if I had any guns at home, and when I said yes, he ordered me to surrender them at once and told me that, given my pending trial, I'd have to stay within 25 miles of home unless I specifically asked for permission to travel.

Outside, I started weeping as Martina and I left the police station, feeling more broken and alone than ever. Martina was quiet and patted my arm. "Don't worry. You're not going to jail," she said, but still, I felt like I was suffocating and it was difficult to walk. Each leg felt like it weighed a thousand pounds as I followed her back to the car.

Maybe this was the bottom. Maybe I've really hit it now, I thought as we started driving back to Monroe from Chicago. Martina was behind the wheel because I was in no fit state to drive.

Just before we reached the toll stop in Freeport, my phone rang. It was Pedro. I angled my face toward the window so Martina couldn't see my expression as I asked Pedro about the peppers. "How's the farm?" I said. "Are the *chiles* red or green?" Naturally I was hoping he'd say we'd had the best crop of peppers, and they were green.

Instead, there was a brief, choked silence. Then Pedro said, "I'm sorry, Miguel, but the *chiles* aren't green. They're already red."

"Holy shit," I said, and hung up. I turned back to Martina. "You're cheating on me with Alejandro!"

"*¿Que?* Don't be ridiculous," she said, but her knuckles were white on the steering wheel.

"Stop the car!" I shouted.

"*¿Que?* Why? Miguel, you're hysterical."

"I said stop the car. I'm going to puke!"

She wheeled into the McDonald's parking lot at the rest stop, and I threw open the car door. I climbed out and threw up in the grass, my sides heaving, my vision blurring so that all I saw was the Black man from the jail and that shuffling line of people. I was going to jail, and Martina was cheating on me. My life was over.

Betrayal

The chest pains started then, and I was certain I was having a heart attack. I couldn't breathe, and my vision was going black. I fell to my knees and then sat on the curb, forcing air in and out of my lungs until at last I was able to stand up again. Tears poured down my face.

Martina was still in the car, both hands frozen on the steering wheel. "*¿Estas bien?*"

"How can you even ask me that? Of course I'm not all right." I found a napkin in the glove compartment and wiped my face. "Just drive."

At home, I paced the halls, my emotions clawing at my chest. My mind was spinning out of control, and I had no outlet for that swirling red cloud of anger. Seeking relief, I began drinking any sort of alcohol I could get my hands on: beers and wine from the fridge, whiskey from the bar. At one point I ran, weeping, into Cristobal's bedroom and shouted, "Your *madre* been cheating on me! She's a *puta*!"

Next, I ran into our bedroom, frantically tearing up Martina's clothes, destroying them in a blind fury because I couldn't hurt her. Martina had given up screaming at me and took the kids away, all three of them looking shocked and terrified. I'd always been such a patient husband and father that to them I'm sure I looked like The Transformer my father had been to me.

Finally, the house couldn't contain me any longer. I fled, grabbing the first car keys I saw—the keys to Cristobal's red Audi—and sped out of the driveway. We had a long, tree-lined driveway, and I gunned the engine at the final curve. The rear wheels skidded, and the car bucked into gear. I lost control at that point, and the Audi slammed into a tree, smashing the driver's door and setting off the airbags. The car had landed in the ditch next to the driveway and was good and stuck, the wheels spinning in place when I tried to drive it out of there.

The House that Cheese Built

Despite the amount of alcohol I'd consumed, I still had enough presence of mind to realize it would be a bad idea to drive a smashed-up car on the highway and attract the notice of the police. I ran back to the house, started up our tractor, and used that and a chain to haul the Audi out of the ditch.

I drove the car back to the house and then sped down the driveway again, this time on my motorcycle. Again, I had just barely enough consciousness not to kill myself. I stopped at the hotel closest to our house, a rundown Motel 6, to sleep off my drink and fury after crying myself to sleep.

When I woke up the next day, I swallowed some of the wretched motel coffee and climbed back on the motorcycle. To my shock, it wouldn't start, no matter what I did. What the hell could have happened to the bike overnight?

I began glumly walking the motorcycle along the road, walking toward town with the vague idea of taking the bike to a mechanic who might figure out the problem. I'd probably been walking for half an hour when a truck pulled up beside me. The driver was Kevin Weiss, my friend from Klondike.

"Hey, Miguel," he called. "What's up? What's the problem?"

Where to begin? I had so many problems on my mind that all I could do was shake my head at him and say, "I don't know. The bike just doesn't want to start."

"Here, let me have a look." Kevin parked his truck on the side of the road and fiddled with the key in the motorcycle's ignition. It jumped to life almost immediately. "You engaged the kill switch, Miguel," he said in confusion. "Why'd you do that?"

I'd been so deep in my pain, walking and thinking, that this simple solution had never even occurred to me. Now I felt like an idiot—a depressed idiot. "I'm not thinking straight," I said. "I just found out Martina's been cheating on me."

199

Betrayal

"What?" Kevin said in shock. "Oh, man. Come on. Drive to my house. You look like you could use a beer."

The last thing I needed was more alcohol, but I was so grateful for his company that I did as he said. Within minutes I was sitting in Kevin's kitchen with a beer in my hand, spilling my guts. He was divorced, and had been for a long time, so Kevin understood the pain of a marriage breaking up. His suggestion to me was this: "If you still love her, you've got to at least try and work it out, man. Forgive her and ask if she'll take you back."

This was a big ask—it was a tough thing, to swallow my pride about Martina sleeping with somebody else—but I knew Kevin was right, so I resolved to do exactly that. There is a very thin line between love and hate in life, and if I couldn't learn how to control my emotions better, they'd end up killing me. It still hurt me to see Martina, but if I could understand this key lesson, maybe there was hope for us yet.

Back home, I was relieved to see that Martina had returned with the kids. "We need to talk," I said.

She wouldn't meet my eyes. "There's nothing to talk about, Miguel. I didn't do what you said, but you won't believe me. You acted like *un idiota* yesterday. I'm through with you."

Never had I felt so low. I was totally lost. I started screaming at her. "Why are you doing this to me?"

She continued denying everything. "I'm telling you, *nada* happened with Alejandro," she said.

"I know you're lying!" I shouted, then broke down in tears. "I need you, Martina! Why are you fucking up our *familia* by going after some guy and fucking him? You broke my fucking heart!" I dropped to my knees. "Please, please don't leave me," I begged. "I'm nothing without you. I don't care that you slept with somebody else. I want to know what I can do to win you back."

Martina still wouldn't look at me. Instead, she pulled off her wedding ring and threw it onto the floor. "No. It's over," she said. "I'm free." She walked out of the kitchen without looking back.

I ran after her, but she drove away. I found Tuti in her room and told her what had happened. "I'm sorry you had to see me like that yesterday," I said. "I made a mistake. I love your *madre,* and she hurt me. I was very jealous."

"I know, Dad," she said quietly.

I found Cristobal next. "I'm sorry for how I behaved," I said. "I'll buy you another car."

He shook his head at me, clearly still pissed off. "Just leave, Dad."

"How can I leave?" I pleaded. "I'm scared about this lawsuit. You don't understand how insecure I feel. I don't write well in English, and I've hardly ever handled our finances. What will I do without your *madre?*"

"I don't know," Cristobal said, "but you're an idiot if you stay."

And so I left.

■ ■ ■

Until recently, I'd been certain I was at the pinnacle of my life, with a good business and a loving family. What was left for me now? I was restricted from traveling more than 25 miles from Monroe, according to my court agreement, so there was no place for me to go. The police had come to search my house for weapons, and I'd surrendered them all. The kids were busy with their own activities. And now Martina—my heart, my breath, my everything—had left me.

The image of the enormous Black man in handcuffs and ankle chains jumped out at me from every shadow. I was terrified that I'd die in prison, and that nobody would even care, including me. Who was I, without Martina?

Betrayal

When Martina came back to the house, I again begged her to stay with me. "Please, please stay with me, Martina. I am nothing without you!"

"Miguel, I can't live like this," she said. "Stop."

We continued fighting until she got scared and left again, taking the kids with her. I didn't blame her. Still, in my frustration at not being able to get Martina to stay with me, my fury rose until again I was in that blood-red state of rage. This time I took my anger out on the family photographs. I grabbed a can of orange spray paint out of the garage and spray-painted over every family picture hanging on the walls.

Then, desperate for solace, searching for anything to numb the pain, I rummaged in the bathroom cabinet and found a bottle of Unisom. Martina took sleeping pills sometimes when she suffered from insomnia; this was a fairly full bottle. I swallowed the pills without thinking, counting each one as I gulped it down: 36 tablets in all. Then I went back downstairs to the basement—the only part of the house that truly felt like mine—and lay down, hoping I'd taken enough to kill me.

"I will die in my basement in silence," I muttered, and within minutes I felt it happening: my limbs grew heavy, and I could no longer turn my head. My body felt like it was made of cement.

Just before falling asleep, I felt totally stupid and furious with myself. First of all, I was angry for having allowed myself to be such a dumbass worker, doing nothing but work for most of my life, and all for a woman who ultimately betrayed me. How could I have allowed myself to grow so dependent on Martina?

I was infuriated with myself as well. What had I done, taking those pills? What would happen if I did die and my kids found me here? What trauma would they suffer? I'd worked hard to be the best father and provider I could be, but now I was letting them down after all, just as my own father had let me down and just as Juan had traumatized his family by shooting himself.

I felt like crying, but I was too numb from the pills to shed any more tears. All I could do was let my eyelids slam shut.

When I woke up, it was like coming out of a deep anesthesia, swimming to consciousness. My stomach roiled, and I vomited, then felt so dehydrated that I drank some water. When was the last time I'd eaten? I couldn't remember; I made a sandwich and called the lawyers at Katten to tell them what I'd done. There was nobody else I could think of who might help me.

"I need to move," I said.

"What do you mean?" asked Dan, the lawyer who'd answered my call.

"I mean out of my house. Martina and I need some time apart. Can you get the judge to grant me permission to move to Chicago?"

My brother Joaquin came to stay with me in Wisconsin for a few days while Martina was in Mexico. There wasn't much we could do, since I was prohibited from traveling more than 25 miles until my attorneys worked something out and I was allowed to move to Chicago. We mostly exercised, hiking the trails I'd made on our property. It was painful for me not to be able to travel to my favorite fishing spots or shooting range because they were too far away.

One day, we were riding stationary bikes at the gym in Monroe when Joaquin was telling me that he'd touched bottom as an alcoholic, which had led him to join Alcoholics Anonymous. "What you need to do is touch bottom and change your personality, Miguel."

"I've never been an *alcoholico*," I said, "and I don't think I could change my personality."

Finally things were settled, and Joaquin helped me move into an apartment my lawyers found for me in Chicago. My brother had really tried to support me through my depression, and I appreciated that. When it was time for Joaquin to leave, however, he asked me for 600,000 pesos to start a new business of his own in Mexico.

I could have afforded to give this money to him despite the monstrous attorney bills mounting up, but I was floored by Joaquin's decision to grasp greedily at my bank account while I was so vulnerable. Besides, I had helped him many times before, starting with that decision to hire him to drive my cheese truck all those years ago, and he'd tried to steal from me then, too. Money, it turns out, really is the devil when it comes to complicating relationships with loved ones.

"You know what, Joaquin," I said, "I'm going to say no. Thank you for coming to help me, and I appreciate your honesty in telling me now that you want something in exchange for your support, but please never come back here again if your intent is to ask me for more *dinero*."

He left, and then I really was alone, living high above the city in a beautiful but lonely golden cage. My new apartment in Chicago was a clean, spare place on the 44th floor of a building by the lake, in an area they call "The Viagra Triangle" because it's thick with wealthy older men like me. There was plenty of action—bars, restaurants, clubs—but I didn't really have the heart for it. I was still too hung up on Martina.

I did try to go out and find company to take my mind off the trial, but it was difficult. There were plenty of beautiful women who expressed an interest in me—or at least in my money, if I'm honest—and I slept with some of them. Truthfully, though, whenever I made love to another woman, I felt horrible. Martina and I had filed for separation, but we weren't divorced yet, so it still felt like I was cheating on her.

I tried numbing my pain with alcohol, too, but discovered that alcohol only makes you more depressed and makes your head hurt. Drinking never helped me forget anything. If you get to the bottom of a tequila bottle, you'll only find more sadness. I continued

The House that Cheese Built

ruminating on the fact that, within a few seconds, I'd lost everything of value in my life.

A couple of months after moving into the apartment, I was drinking heavily and talking to my brother Carlos on the phone.

"I don't even want to live anymore," I said. "What's the point? Martina has already left me. *Mi ninos* are too busy to spend time with me. And at the end of the day, I'll probably go to prison and die there. What the hell's the point of my existence? So I've decided to end it all. I've cut my wrists."

It was true: I'd sliced my wrists with a kitchen knife and was watching the blood seep out while talking to my brother. Carlos said something I couldn't understand because the tequila had me in its grip. My eyelids were too heavy to hold open, and my head sank into my chest. I passed out with the phone receiver cradled beneath my chin.

I woke to pounding sounds in my head, only it turned out that the pounding was real: the police were at my door. Carlos had called my friend Jorge, who in turn tried my cell phone multiple times. When I didn't pick up, Jorge had called the police and asked them to do a wellness check at my apartment.

I refused to sign any papers to be admitted to a hospital voluntarily. This was a mistake, as it turned out, because they gave me a sedative and took me by ambulance to the psych unit of a downtown hospital, where I was admitted to a locked ward because I'd been deemed a danger to myself. I was wearing pajamas and didn't have any identification papers on me.

The sedative wore off at last by mid-morning. When I woke up, I was in a double room with a young Black guy. The door was locked from the outside. When I pounded on it in a panic, a nurse came and informed me that I'd have to stay in the hospital until the psychiatrist in charge of the unit returned from vacation.

"And how long will that be?" I asked in horror.

"About two weeks. He just left, I'm afraid."

"Can't I see anyone else? I need to get out of here!"

"Mr. Leal, we've admitted you because you tried to take your own life," the nurse said patiently. "We think it's best that you stay until you get the help you need."

"But I'm not crazy! I promise that I'm not going to commit suicide. I wasn't that serious about doing it!"

"Two weeks," she repeated. The nurse was already leaving the room, hurrying to see another patient.

"Hold on!" I shouted after her. "Don't I have the right to make a phone call or something? You can't just lock me in here against my will!"

She turned around and sighed. "Yes, Mr. Leal, you can certainly make a phone call. I will help you place it. Who do you wish to call?"

One of the people I called to tell about my involuntary hospital stay was my friend Marta; we'd been involved on and off since my divorce, and she was one of the few people I was close to in Chicago, since my social life had previously consisted of people I knew at work and Martina. I wondered if Martina and the children even knew where I was—or whether they'd care if they did. This was such a terrible thought that I called my attorneys and told them what had happened.

"You need to get me out of here," I said.

"Of course. Let me work on it," Dan said.

A short while later, however, he called me back with bad news. "Listen, you can't leave until you're evaluated, Miguel. You tried to commit suicide, so you're considered a danger to yourself until we can get a psychiatrist to clear you for leaving the unit."

I begged, yelled, and pleaded my case, but it was no use. The law was the law, Dan told me. "I'm sure the doctor will see you and realize there's been a mistake," he said, in a tone that I recognized as placating. Dan probably thought I was crazy, too.

"He's not coming back for two weeks!" I said. "How do you expect me to stay here that long?"

"It's out of my hands, Miguel. Try to get some rest. I'm sorry."

Not as sorry as I was. I slammed down the receiver, and the nurse took the phone away, shaking her head.

During my time in the psychiatric hospital, I thought about what Joaquin had said about touching bottom. This, for me, was a bottom I'd never reached before. It was way deeper than I'd thought.

Somehow, I managed to sleep for most of the day, probably because I was so emotionally wrung out. They turned the lights out at ten o'clock every night, and at one point I woke up around 3 a.m., totally disoriented. I didn't know what the hell was going on. Through the window, I saw a light, and wondered if that was the light everyone talked about seeing on their deathbeds. I didn't believe in God, and if there did turn out to be a God, I sure as hell didn't believe He'd have time to pay attention to any of us. I was on my own.

It was lunchtime the next day by the time I felt fully awake again. The aides were coming around with trays of foul looking food: limp sandwiches on white bread with dead looking lettuce, cartons of milk, and apples with soft spots.

I stared at the food in horror. Just before attempting to take my life, I'd been living like a king in one of the toniest areas of Chicago, where I'd eaten in the best restaurants and sipped balloon glasses of expensive wines.

After examining the sandwich on my tray, I dropped it. "Fuck, this is horrible!"

The guy in the bed next to mine was grinning at his own tray. "This is a miracle!" he cried. "I have food!"

Suddenly, it hit me hard that I'd forgotten what hunger was. I'd been able to buy whatever I wanted, whenever I wanted, for so long that I had gotten greedy.

207

Betrayal

I need to put my feet back on the ground, I thought, and turned to the other man. "Would you like my sandwich?" I said.

"You bet, man," he said happily and gobbled it down.

I sank back against the pillows and watched him eat, marveling at his happiness. I'd had everything that should have made me happy: plenty of money, a big house, a wife, and children. I'd been at what I thought was the pinnacle of my life. The problem was that it wasn't *my* life. I'd been living not for myself, but for Martina. All of the choices I'd made up until this point in my life had been made with the goal of making her proud of me and of providing for her and the children.

The thing about truly touching bottom in your life is that, if you're lucky, you find a coffer of gold. That gold is your new understanding of life. Now it dawned on me that I needed a new script. Martina was no longer going to tell me what path to follow. I'd have to do that myself. There was just one problem: I had no idea where to begin, especially because first I'd have to fight a court case and survive jail time if I didn't win.

All I knew with any certainty was that I had been wrong about most things in my life. I had once thought that all I needed to do was win this woman's heart to be happy, to build the family life with her that I'd never had in my own childhood. The family lore—indeed, nearly every immigrant's bible—is that happiness is born of financial success, and I'd taken that to heart as well. Yet, despite marrying the woman I'd always loved and having more money than I knew what to do with, I had been humbled by my mistakes and by the many betrayals I'd experienced.

Today, I am grateful for that humbling. Sometimes we can only reach our full potential when everything is taken away from us, forcing us to look within ourselves for yet more strength to find a new purpose and passion in life. This was yet another point in time where I would need to pay close attention to opportunity if I was ever going to survive my losses and build a new future.

The House that Cheese Built

Chapter 12

Fighting for My Life

To Truly Succeed, Look Within Yourself to Make the Decisions Best for You.

When the psychiatrist returned from his vacation, he met with me for an intensive therapy session. After I'd told him everything about the company, my wife leaving me, and the lawsuit, it became clear to him that I was dealing with a situational depression exacerbated by drinking alcohol.

"You made a serious mistake, Miguel," he said. "Potentially a lethal one."

"It won't happen again," I promised. "I know I need to turn the page and start a new life."

He must have believed me, because the doctor shook my hand and signed the release papers that afternoon.

"Listen," I said, "I want to do something nice for the other patients. The food you have in this hospital is really awful. How about if I send the other patients some steak dinners or something?"

"No, Miguel, sorry," he said. "We can't allow that."

I was devastated. I couldn't imagine being stuck in that hospital, eating whatever shit they handed out on those trays. Still, my spirits perked up when I saw my friends Marta and Ernesto coming toward me around the fountain in the garden, like some kind of scene in a movie with a happy ending, ready to embrace me and get me out of there.

Martina was back in Wisconsin. When I went to see her, to tell her about my suicide attempt, the hospital stay, and how my legal bills were mounting up, she remained cold and unmoved. "You did that to yourself, Miguel," she said. "This legal case has nothing to do with me."

"How can you say that?" I demanded. "You were in charge of the warehouses. You were supervising Cynthia Guttierez, for God's sake. I agree that we don't want both of us going to jail because *los ninos* need us. I'm willing to take responsibility. But the least you can do is help me pay these legal fees. They're in the tens of thousands of dollars now."

"No," she said.

"No?" I was incredulous.

"No," she said. "When are you going to believe me that you're on your own? It's your *problema,* and you're stuck with it. I'm not paying a fucking penny for this lawsuit."

Martina took another trip to Mexico soon after that, saying she had to visit her mother and that she'd be staying at her sister's house. I knew this was most likely a lie; she was probably with her lover. When the kids asked where their mother had gone, I told them the truth. I was fed up with Martina's deception.

My daughter was shocked. "Mom wouldn't do that. She went down to *México* to check on the car wash. She's staying with her sister!"

I handed her the phone. "Here. Let's try a little experiment. Why don't you call your *tia* and ask her if your mom's there. Your aunt won't pick up the phone if I call."

Tuti placed the call, and when Alejandra picked up, my daughter asked to speak with Martina. "I'm looking for *mi madre,*" she said.

"Why are you calling me?" Alejandra asked, puzzled. "Your *madre*'s not here."

Shaken, Tuti looked at me as she said, "Okay, that's fine. Just tell her to call me if you hear from her, okay?"

Tuti hung up and called her mother's cell phone next. I watched, arms folded, knowing what was coming and hating myself for it. But I was angrier at Martina than I'd ever been. On top of everything else my wife had done, I'd just discovered that she had stolen my mother's car.

Martina and I had bought my mother a car the last time we were in Mexico together. Stupidly, I'd let Martina handle the finances and the paperwork, just like she always did. I hadn't given it a thought when Martina put the car in her own name. So, when Martina showed up to take the car away from my mother, there wasn't a damn thing I could do about it. The car was in Martina's name, and the police would see that if I reported that the car was stolen. Still, as much as I desperately wanted my daughter to know that I was telling her the truth about Martina cheating on me, I felt terrible. Martina's betrayal of our marriage was bound to break the children's hearts as well as my own.

Martina picked up the phone. I was standing close enough to Tuti in the kitchen to hear her voice. "Hi honey! ¿*Que pasa*?" Martina asked. "Everything okay at home?"

"Yes," Tuti said. "I'm fine. I just wanted to find out where you are."

"But you know where I am, honey," Martina said. "I'm here with your *Tía* Alejandra."

Tuti flushed red with anger. "No, you're not. Quit lying! I just called her, and she says you're not there! You're cheating on *Papa*, aren't you!?" she shouted, and hung up, then fled the kitchen, weeping.

I stood there in the sudden silence, awash with shame that somehow my family was falling apart and I hadn't been able to hold it together.

■ ■ ■

It was looking increasingly likely that I would face jail time. I made up my mind to get into the best possible physical shape before that happened. Maybe that way I'd be able to defend myself better against assaults in jail, or even deter people from trying to attack me.

When I asked a friend for advice about what sort of strength training might build up my speed and fitness level as fast as possible, he suggested something I'd never heard of before: Krav Maga. There was a studio close to our house in Monroe, so I had signed up for classes there. Now that I was living in Chicago, I was determined to find another studio in the city. It's no exaggeration to say that Krav Maga saved my life.

Krav Maga isn't a traditional type of martial arts, but a self-defense system developed by a native Hungarian, Imi Lichtenfeld, an experienced boxer who joined Nazi resistance groups in Europe during WWII. He eventually immigrated to Israel, with a vision of spreading the hand-to-hand combat techniques of Krav Maga throughout the world so people could feel safe enough to "walk in peace." Today, thousands of people train each year at Krav Maga centers worldwide.

My goal in learning Krav Maga was to push myself to the edge of my physical endurance. Life had punched me in the face. Now I wanted to learn how to punch back.

The instructor, Hike, was from Russia. He trained me hard until I was in the best physical condition of my life. At the same time, I learned how to defend myself against strikes, chokes, punches, and headlocks. I also mastered fighting stances and movement skills. As the weeks went by, I was able to effectively punch and kick from both standing and ground positions.

As my body gradually transformed, my mind did, too. Training in martial arts—like many other types of exercise—can impact not only your physical health, but your mental well-being. It helped me feel more confident because I knew how to defend myself. Always before, I had relied too much on Martina to feel secure. Krav Maga taught me how to keep my feet on the ground, both physically and mentally.

I took group Krav Maga classes several times a week with Hike and eventually signed up for his private lessons. There was one truly awful moment. One part of the training is to be blindfolded, and then your opponent chokes you while you try to defend yourself. I began to panic when I was being attacked in the dark, and once again The Transformer exploded from inside me. The goal of this exercise is to knock your opponent down, but I knocked the other guy down, pulled the blindfold off, and punched him over and over again, seeing only red in front of me, until Hike restrained me. That's how much anger was in my heart.

Hike kicked me out of the class. "Come back tomorrow, you dumb idiot."

Afterward, I went home and cried. I couldn't stop. It was like I'd lost the ability to control all of my emotions, from rage to sorrow. It wasn't until I stood in the shower that I calmed down, as if a pressure valve had been opened to release all of the emotions boiling inside. What I learned from that incident is that I had to be more aware of the feelings inside me, especially the anger and my depression, or those emotions could kill me.

I had been seeing a therapist since my stay in the psychiatric hospital. When that one left, I saw two others before ending up with Dr. Malek, a psychiatrist in Chicago. When I told him what had happened in Krav Maga, he surprised me by being pleased by my outburst.

"You're starting to see exactly why you need to stay on top of your emotions, Miguel," he said, and asked me to start recording my emotions and my dreams, too.

Little by little, between Dr. Malek, Krav Maga, and Hike's mentorship, I began to feel calmer and healthier. Engaging in such an extreme training regime meant I had to give up alcohol and eat healthier foods so I could keep up with the practices; this was easy because I was so exhausted from working out that I started going to bed earlier and sleeping better, which, Dr. Malek explained, would keep my mind healthier. My body was always sore, but my mind was calm, so it was worth it.

Various studies have shown that those who engage in martial arts training often experience mental health benefits as well as physical ones. Physical exercise of any sort is often a mood booster—the body produces "feel good" chemicals like endorphins when you engage in exercise.

Beyond that, though, people who practice martial arts often report feeling more confident about who they are and their purpose in life. This is probably because, in Krav Maga and most other martial arts classes, you must master your mind and your emotions, or your opponent will take advantage of your weakness.

"Unstuck" is probably the best word to describe what happened to me. After practicing Krav Maga regularly, I started feeling stronger—strong enough to release my anger not only physically, but emotionally. I had been manipulated by Martina for years. In a way, I'd been like a bird in a gilded cage—a bird that kept insisting on returning to the same place even after the cage was gone because that's where I'd always gotten my food.

Now, though, I began feeling more mentally and physically fit. Awakened. I became increasingly certain that I had more to contribute in this life. With Krav Maga training, I was developing the strength and confidence to fly out of that gilded cage on my own. Eventually I got a tattoo of a large eagle with the words Naci Libre, to remind myself I was born free and should always fly like an eagle.

Still, when my brother Carlos suggested that he come to Chicago to offer me emotional support and help me with the legal case, I accepted eagerly. I still felt lonely, especially at night, without the routines of work and family life.

Carlos came to live with me in the apartment for about four months. It was wonderful to have him there at first. He was an entertaining

214

companion, and we shared so much family history that we understood each other's references and jokes as only siblings can. It was Carlos, too, who made me see the light regarding the lawyers at Katten.

"Really, Miguel, what have those guys done for you?" Carlos fumed after one long, pointless meeting with the attorneys. "They've milked you for over a million bucks, and from what I can see, they've given you nothing for that money. They've got absolutely no clear defensive strategy worked up for you. Break up with them, already!"

With Carlos backing me up, I began complaining to Katten about their fees—one month I got a bill for $90,000, and another for $120,000—and telling them outright that I saw no reason for them to charge me that much money when they clearly weren't making any progress in getting the case thrown out.

"I mean, it's not like you're defending O.J. Simpson here, guys," I said. "So why are you charging me these celebrity prices? I don't want to be with you anymore!"

At last Katten had no choice but to listen. They passed me on to another attorney, David Weisman. He was young, but sharp, and agreed to represent me for $80,000—a drop in the bucket compared to what Katten was charging me. I was so relieved by changing lawyers, and so eager to have the whole case behind me, that when Dave suggested I plead guilty and take a plea bargain, I actually considered doing it. I just wanted this whole nightmare to be over.

"There's just one thing, Dave," I said. "I did nothing wrong. How can I declare myself guilty, when it was Cynthia who told the FDA that the papers were legal? Her boyfriend, Tony, was the one who falsified those papers so the cincho cheese would pass inspection."

Dave frowned. "The thing is, Miguel, there are compromising emails between you and this José Zurita guy. He asked if you could help him substitute those 311 boxes of cincho cheese in case the FDA agents came looking for them, and you agreed. I know you never actually changed the boxes or tried to hide anything from the

Fighting for My Life

inspectors, but the FDA has those emails. They can use them against you to prove there was a conspiracy and you're trying to cover it up. See what I mean? You have to admit you're guilty before we can ask for a plea bargain."

I felt pushed into a corner, and I was suffocating under the pressure of having this case weigh on my chest for the past three years. "All right. Do what you have to do. Let's enter a guilty plea. Just finish this thing, please. I need to get my life back."

■ ■ ■

Gradually, as the investigation continued and I grew stronger after my hospital stay and less shell-shocked about the investigation, it became clear to me that Martina might have been right about Carlos: he was spending my money like it was his own, manipulating me to give him "living expenses" any chance he got.

Finally, I had no choice but to ask him to leave. "I don't know what your intent was in coming here, Carlos, but I think I'd be better off without you."

At that point, Carlos showed his true colors, arranging a meeting with a lawyer and trying to strong-arm me into signing a contract that would guarantee that I'd pay him the ludicrous sum of $20,000 monthly for the rest of his life—all because he'd come to the United States to help me out for four months! Again, I was struck by how greedy and self-centered my brothers were. Never again would I trust them.

■ ■ ■

As my trial date loomed, I was also in the process of divorcing Martina. We had officially been separated for three years, and she was spending most of her time in Mexico now that the kids were out of the house—both of them off to college in Denver, Colorado.

I hadn't spoken to Cristobal since our last quarrel. I felt bad about that, but he wouldn't respond to my calls or emails. Since Martina had left the country, my attorney assured me that I could proceed with finalizing the divorce if I gave her power of attorney and sent her to the Mexican embassy to sign the papers, which my attorney did.

Soon after that, I told Martina we either had to sell the house or she had to buy me out; at least that would help offset my astronomical attorney fees. She tried to weasel her way out of it, claiming we weren't divorced yet, so she didn't have to pay me anything. However, I sent her a certified letter with a copy of the divorce agreement, and she had no choice but to capitulate.

Once Martina had paid for her share of the house, I drove back to Monroe, Wisconsin, for the last time. It was a sad homecoming. The house had been shut up for months because Martina was in Mexico and the kids were gone. It was dusty, damp, and unloved. My footsteps echoed in the hallways as I roamed from room to room, growing increasingly depressed and angry as I gathered family photographs, papers, clothing, and anything else that held memories of our time together, and made a huge pile in the backyard.

There was a safe in the house, but I couldn't remember the combination, so I called some friends from Monroe and told them to force it open, which they did, making a huge hole in the safe so I could extract the passports and other family papers. I left a note for Martina, saying, "I don't need you anymore, you *pinche* bitch, I can take care of myself."

I went back outside to that pile of family belongings and memories and set them ablaze. I stood there watching my family life burst into flames and turn to ashes, crying and shivering in the night air. Losing my family life had hurt so much, I had no choice but to destroy these memories, hoping that might release me from the pain.

■ ■ ■

217

Fighting for My Life

About six months after my first meeting with Dave Weisman, I went in front of the judge and entered my guilty plea.

"Do you understand what you're saying?" the judge asked. "That you're saying you're guilty?"

"Yes," I said, but I was lying. I still didn't agree with Dave that pleading guilty was the right way to go. Much, much later, in reflecting on those emails, I realized I had never actually agreed to any plan of Jose Zurita's; my responses to him had all consisted of questions. How did that make me guilty?

In retrospect, I certainly wish I'd handled many steps of this litigation differently. If I hadn't been so gullible, I probably would have switched attorneys sooner in the process, and I certainly wouldn't have let my love for Martina cloud my judgment. Once again, however, I was learning valuable lessons here.

One of my most valuable takeaways was that, whether you're up and your business is growing well, or you're down and struggling to come back from losses or mistakes in judgment, you must maintain your physical health as a way to protect your mental health. Practicing Krav Maga gave me an outlet for my anger and made me confident enough to survive not only through my depression, but this tedious, terrifying legal battle. In the process, I was also finding my new identity as a man who is confident enough to make his own decisions without a partner by his side—something I should have learned long before this point in my life.

Chapter 13

Four Days in Court

Be Honest, and People Will Believe in You.

Our first trial date was set for June 12, 2014, some seven years after the original call from the FDA. In the courtroom, I listened to Gabriel Plotkin's opening statements—he was defending me, along with David Weisman, and I could scarcely breathe, I was so nervous.

Imagine being in a room where your fate is completely in someone else's hands, knowing you're innocent, but the judge could declare you guilty and send you to jail for months, or even years. The stress was nearly intolerable.

I was seated up front near the judge; the only thing that made my situation bearable was glancing over my shoulder and seeing my family gathered—everyone but my brother Joaquin, who couldn't get a visa, and Cristobal—and feeling their love and support.

Breathe deeply, I reminded myself. *You're not what the government is trying to say you are.*

"Mr. Leal has pled guilty to a crime," Gabriel began. "He entered a plea agreement in which he admitted that in April 2007, over a period of five days, he agreed with his co-defendants to lie to the FDA. He agreed to lie about the location of 311 boxes of imported cincho cheese that he had already sold because he thought he had permission to sell it.

"Specifically, Mr. Leal agreed to tell the FDA that these 311 boxes of cheese were in his plant in Darlington, Wisconsin, if the FDA ever asked. And he agreed to place 311 boxes of substitute cheese in his Darlington plant if the FDA ever came looking for it.

"As it turns out, the FDA never did ask Mr. Leal about the cheese, and the FDA never did go to his plant in Darlington to look for the cincho cheese, but the FDA did meet with his co-defendants. And his agreement to participate in their lie was and is a crime. He's pled guilty to that conduct, and he is here before the court to accept his punishment."

Gabriel went on to point out that the government refused to accept that this was all I'd done wrong, however, and was trying to try to prove that "another, more sinister crime has taken place. In short, the government believes that the April agreement was only a small part of an otherwise much grander criminal scheme. A scheme to knowingly sell adulterated cheese into the stream of commerce for months on end."

He added that the FDA had done tests on the cheese to prove it was "adulterated," or contaminated with harmful bacteria. Based on those tests, the government was going to "inordinate lengths" to prove that I knew this fact, and that my agreement to lie about where the missing cheese was had to be part of a larger conspiracy to hide that fact.

"While these FDA tests occurred," Gabriel went on, "the government has admitted and will admit there's no evidence that Mr. Leal ever received the test results. And while the FDA chased the producer of the cheese throughout the summer of 2007, issuing hold orders and destruction orders for the cincho cheese, the court will hear no evidence, because there is none, that Mr. Leal ever received those orders."

And that, in a nutshell, was my defense: that I hadn't ever received any information about the cheese being contaminated. Would it be enough to keep me out of jail?

My hopes rose when I heard Gabriel outline what a US probation officer familiar with the case, Sandy DeNicholas, had concluded. "She poured over a number of case-related documents, and she interviewed the lead case agent for this investigation, Special Agent Ronnie Melham," Gabriel said. "From all of this, she concluded that the crime was narrow and spanned a few days, that there was no actual or intended loss, there were no victims, there were no sophisticated means employed, and Mr. Leal was no organizer or leader. Rather, Jose Zurita was. And she concluded that the appropriate guideline range in this case is 10 to 16 months."

I didn't want to spend any time at all in prison, of course. But even 16 months was a lot better than the 19-year jail sentence Melham had been proposing. For a moment, I allowed my shoulders to relax a notch. Maybe I could survive this after all.

■ ■ ■

Our next day in court wasn't until October 27, 2014, due to scheduling issues with some of the witnesses. The day went well for my defense, with David Weisman reminding the judge that the government would stipulate there was "no evidence of any physical injury as a result of the cheese at issue in this case," and that the government would also admit there was no evidence that I, or anyone in my company, had ever received evidence of FDA testing.

When we reconvened on October 30, Renato Mariotti represented the FDA. My heart sank at the sight of him. He had vowed to put me in jail for a good portion of my life. Would he succeed? Again, I had to force myself to breathe deeply and to look over my shoulder now and then at my friends and family so I wouldn't feel so alone.

David Weisman started the day by reminding the judge that I'd pled guilty to the crime of agreeing with Cynthia Guittierez and Jose Zurita that I would hide 311 boxes of cincho cheese in my plant if the FDA ever asked and substitute them with other boxes of cheese.

David also reminded the court that the FDA had never actually gone out to the warehouse to meet with me, only with my co-defendants.

"His agreement to participate in their lie was and is a crime," David said of me. "He's pled guilty to that conduct, and he is here before the court to accept his punishment." The reason we couldn't simply proceed to sentencing, he added, was because "the government wants more. The government refuses to accept that this is all Mr. Leal has done wrong and insists on calling witnesses to try to prove that another more sinister crime has taken place."

The day went on from there, with long descriptions by my own attorneys of cincho cheese and of my company. They also detailed how I'd bought the cincho cheese from Jose Zurita over many months, most recently in April, May, and June 2007. The government's side— Renato—then called witnesses for the prosecution, starting with their microbiologist and consumer safety officer, who testified about the government's general safety sampling procedures. She said some samples of the cincho cheese we'd imported tested positive for E. coli, an indication of fecal contamination, and other bacteria.

The day dragged on, with various witnesses talking about cheese making of both hard and soft cheeses, raw milk cheeses versus cheeses made with pasteurized milk, and how the cheese we'd bought didn't all come from the same Mexican factory, but from various small cheesemakers who all had their own processes. The technical talk went on for so long that the judge decided we needed another day for the government's witnesses. He adjourned the court around 4 p.m., which meant I had another sleepless night ahead of me, waiting for my fate to be determined by the court.

As I left the courtroom, I stopped in the men's room. Just as I finished washing my hands and was leaving the bathroom, Ron Melham appeared. I held the door open and blocked his exit for a minute, staring him down. This guy knew the truth. He knew Martina had been in charge of paying the invoices and working with Cynthia;

he must have known she was setting me up by saying she had nothing to do with the warehouse, when in fact she was Cynthia's direct supervisor.

"Why did you do this to me, Ron?" I asked. "You know I didn't do anything wrong, yet you cost me my family for this. And you call yourself a Catholic? I don't know how you live with yourself."

His face turned completely white, but Ron didn't say a word. I shook my head and moved aside to let him enter the bathroom. Ron pushed past me without a word.

■ ■ ■

It was Renato's turn, still, to call witnesses the next day. He studiously avoided glancing my way as he called his first witness, the deputy district director of the FDA, who informed the court about various FDA procedures and what they meant, like putting a product on hold status due to risk. He also talked about being asked to find where the cheese had entered, and said that the full shipment was available for review in Chicago, where he went to our warehouse to see the cheese matching the description of the cincho put on hold by the FDA. He'd received paperwork from Cynthia, this witness said, and was told that all of the cheese had been sold.

When David Weisman cross-examined this government witness, he pointed out (to my relief) that the consignee listed on the form wasn't our company, Mexican Cheese Producers, but Hot Peppers, Inc. (HPI), Jose Zurita's company, which had brought the cheese across the border and supposedly held it for inspection. David again reminded the court that I was being held accountable "for things he has no idea about, and the reason he has no idea about it is because someone *else* was lying to the FDA."

Cynthia took the stand late in the afternoon and discussed her own duties—inventory and accounts receivable and payable. She also admitted, I was happy to hear, that Martina was supervising her responsibilities.

223

Cynthia was a witness for the government's side. Under cross-examination by Gabriel, he made it clear that our company had not gone down to Mexico to get the cheese and bring it across the border; rather, HPI, Jose Zurita's company, was responsible for clearing customs and getting an FDA release. By the time the cheese showed up at our warehouse, all of the papers should have been signed, showing it had been inspected by the FDA and was ready to sell. Gabriel also explained to the court that Cynthia had made a plea agreement with the FDA, and part of that agreement was that she'd testify against me. In exchange, the government had allowed Cynthia—who had no citizenship papers yet—to remain in the United States for the years between the investigation and the trial and continue to work.

What's more, Gabriel got Cynthia to admit, under oath, that she had never actually told me that the FDA inspector had said we couldn't sell the cheese in question. Nor had she ever received an email from me saying, "Let's sell the cheese anyway." Most importantly, Cynthia told the court that it was Jose Zurita's idea to create a fake bill of lading that could be sent to the FDA—and that I was never copied on any of those emails.

I could suddenly breathe more easily. Surely the judge would hear this testimony and realize I was innocent?

■ ■ ■

Two weeks later, on November 21, 2014, we were back in court, where my attorneys showed the judge a document stipulating "a number of things where the government has said there is no evidence of something," like the fact that I'd received orders from the FDA to hold the cincho cheese or knew of lab reports showing the cheese would be dangerous to consume.

In addition, Gabriel said the document he was presenting "impeaches by omission testimony by Ms. Gutierrez on the stand. . . . She said on the stand that she told Mr. Leal in April that the FDA inspector who came to visit DQM didn't want them to sell the cincho cheese. This reflects that she had not previously said that in her five formal interviews with Special Agent Malham."

My attorneys went on to point out that it was Jose Zurita, not me, who was managing and supervising Cynthia and the others, like his brother Tony. He told them what to do with the cheese, like which pallets to set aside for the FDA and how to create a fake bill of lading. My lawyers repeated their assertion that I had no knowledge of this, since I was never copied on any of the emails.

"Zurita," said Gabriel, "is the organizer and leader behind what is going on here."

The last bit of evidence my attorneys produced was an email from me to Jose Zurita, sent on July 3, saying "I'm done buying cheese from you." This was significant because the government agents were suggesting that bad cheese was going out through July, August, and September.

"It's not true," my attorneys said adamantly. "No cincho cheese left DQM after July 26th of 2007."

In conclusion, my attorneys said this: "The government has suggested that bad cheese was being distributed into September, and that certain things learned in August, the end of August, should have told . . . Mr. Leal that the cheese was adulterated and he shouldn't have continued to sell it. But what this reflects is that they didn't know about any problems of mold of any significance until June 27. On July 3 he said, 'I'm not buying anymore,' and by July 26 no more cheese was being distributed by DQM. He says, at the top here, it's been over a month without having clean cheese, cheese that went through and survived this washing process, that I can sell."

There was more—much more—said in my defense that day, including the mention of a woman named Maria Castro, of Castro Cheese in Texas, who had bought the cincho from Jose Zurita after I told Jose I didn't want any more of it. Maria Castro had sold the cincho cheese despite there being a hold order from the FDA on the cincho. Castro had told the FDA that Zurita had said "the cheese would be tested by FDA and meet all legal requirements before it came to us as it was happening with Mexican Cheese Producers in Wisconsin."

Toward the end of the day, my attorneys pulled one more card out of their sleeve. This time it was a report by an expert cheese-maker attesting to the fact that I had "shown a strong commitment to food safety." This report highlighted the fact that I'd tested all of my cheese samples through Silliker Laboratories, "one of the best micro-biological testing laboratories in the United States." The expert noted that the testing is expensive and not required by law, showing "the commitment of MCP and Mr. Leal to assure the safety of the products he produced."

My stomach dropped into my shoes when the judge said he was ready to sentence me the next time we met. I could scarcely listen when my attorneys wrapped up their case, pleading with the judge on my behalf to throw out the government's determined efforts to make me serve jail time for a minimum of 9 to 11 years, and perhaps more.

David Weisman made a defense on my behalf, concluding with a speech that nearly made me weep because it laid out my situation so plainly. "Judge," he began, "Mr. Leal has been sitting for seven years with this case on his shoulders. He attempted to take his own life prior to this plea agreement . . . the fact of the matter is, the government was seeking 15 years of his life and that is part of the reason why he attempted to take his own life."

This was it. The trial was over. The next time we met in court, the judge would hand down my sentence. It would be the end of my freedom. But for how long?

■ ■ ■

We didn't have another court date until May 8, 2015. I tried to put aside my worries about the possible jail time I'd have to serve by keeping busy with Krav Maga classes, preparing myself for whatever, or whoever, might await me in prison. I was eating better, drinking less, and, consequently, sleeping better. I'd had a girlfriend for a time but ended the relationship because I wasn't ready for the level of commitment she expected from me. I remained, for the most part, a loner.

The cloudy weather reflected my mood as I arrived at the courthouse on that last day before the judge. I was already sweating from the humidity even though the temperature hadn't hit 80 degrees yet. My hands trembled too hard for me to grasp the glass of water poured for me when I sat down, so I rested them on my thighs beneath the table and waited for the judge to appear.

We rose as he entered the courtroom, as we always did, then sat down and waited for the verdict that would determine how my life would be lived in the next few months—or dozen years. The judge reviewed the documents in front of him—my "pleading," as they called it, and a letter from my psychiatrist, along with the government's suggestions for my sentencing. Then he looked around the courtroom and said he basically agreed with the probation officer's structure.

Part of the difficulty in sentencing me (along with Cynthia and Jose), he said, was this: "You're dealing with a product rather than a bunch of people. There is no robbing of banks, there is no violence. There are things that constitute dangers to the public. And the numbers that get attached to that in the guideline are permissible, but I think they're incorrect, because of what it is that exactly we're dealing with, which is a very large amount of cheese and not significant damage to any person."

In other words, if I understood the judge correctly—and this wasn't always easy for me, since I still had trouble understanding

227

Four Days in Court

English if the words came too fast at me or were too complicated—was that the government had argued their case based on the fact that I was part of a conspiracy to import "filthy" cheese, and my actions "might" have caused harm to a large number of people.

However, the judge went on, "This is a case in which I think injury would be very difficult to prove. That it's possible that somebody got sick? Sure. Not sick enough to report it to anybody, but sick."

The government spent more time arguing their case, and then my attorney stepped in when the judge said, "Some of the issue of how wrong it is depends on what the whole enterprise looks like. Do we have answers to this?"

At that point, another of my attorneys, Mr. Durkin, pointed out that the Elmhurst location of our warehouse was separate from our cheese factory, and that the warehouse was run not by me, but by Martina, "which is an emotional issue for Mr. Leal, which we'll get to later." I winced when he said that, but managed to do the calculations in my head when he asked what percentage of my sales were made up by selling cincho cheese.

"About 0.05% in terms of gross sales," I told the Court, reminding myself, once again, of what a risk I'd taken with this cheese, and what a shame it was that such a small, exciting endeavor of mine had somehow gone so badly wrong.

My lawyer went on to spell out the nature of this endeavor to the judge, saying I was not "in the importing business. He was in the manufacturing business. I don't know whether this is clear enough, but it's my understanding that he made his living and built this company by making cheese in Wisconsin . . . and that the cincho cheese he tried to make in Wisconsin any number of times, but it has to be made with unpasteurized milk, which you can't do in Wisconsin or in the United States. So that's why he ended up trying to import it."

The judge seemed to understand this point. In fact, it appeared to me that he was sympathetic, when he said of me, "You have someone who was relatively new to the product, the product is pretty small compared to what he's ordinarily selling, which suggests to me that perhaps one way to look at this is to say, this is not an elaborate crime, it was a very small deal, and a request from somebody to not tell the truth, but while this is happening, he has another relatively large business to attend to and this is not the center of his life . . . he committed a crime, but you start to wonder precisely how deeply wrong, if at all, his mindset was at the time. This is small potatoes for him."

Naturally, the government's agent, Renato, tried to object to this reasoning several times, yet the judge continued to be clear-eyed about my involvement, saying, "Okay. We are now finished with the last piece of the question I asked, which is the degree to which Leal noticed things happening. Remember, I started out about you run a big company, invariably you don't see it all, and you may not see much of it because there's a lot of other things to do. . . . The one thing I don't have from the government is how he would've noticed."

Again, Renato tried to argue that I had full knowledge and was completely to blame for selling this "filthy" cheese, but the judge cut him off, summarizing the case this way: "What he did, he lied to fend off Food and Drug. He wouldn't be the first guy to do that, but I don't think that he was, in a meaningful way, central to the issue of this cheese . . . some of the people he trusted may not be particularly able, maybe just inept."

At this point, the judge asked the government to suggest what sentencing they thought might be appropriate, now that they'd heard what he had to say. My vision started to dim as panic set in. Was the judge really on my side, as I was beginning to think he was? Or would the government somehow persuade him to go for the toughest possible sentence?

It seemed not. When my defense attorney spoke again, he looked directly at me, saying, "I think you will trust me if I say to you that

229

Four Days in Court

I don't think, in 42 years, I've ever seen someone more tortured by a case and the consequences of his behavior and the situation in which he found himself than Mr. Leal."

He added that I was so tortured mentally that I'd spent time in a locked psychiatric ward. "Now, that occurred before his plea, but after he was charged. This case has hung over him like an albatross for years."

I sat back against my hard wooden chair, nodding. This was truer than even he could know.

"He's still tortured by it," my attorney went on in his closing argument. "If I would take his calls every four hours, he would call every four hours, that's what has weighed on him . . . when this investigation started he had a wife, an intact family, and he was about to hit the lottery. This is a guy that started in this cheese business as a Mexican immigrant who swept the floor and cleaned the machines. . . . So he's about to get the American dream and the American dream turns poison on him. . . . I think a fine is certainly appropriate, and I think it's worth discussing; vis-a-vis, your question about the need for incarceration. It would seem to me that it would be more appropriate, under these circumstances, for a fine, and a significant fine . . . I think it's something you could take into account in considering how hard he's already been hit in the wallet for legal fees. I believe it's close to a million dollars, if not more."

Once again, my attorney pointed out to the judge what I already felt deep in my bones, the agony of losing everything I valued: my wife, my main extracurricular passion of competitive shooting, and my business. Hearing all of this was enough to make me want to put my head down on the desk and close my eyes to block everything out. How had I sunk so low? What must the judge, my family, and all of the strangers in this courtroom think of me, now that I was nothing?

In the end, the judge wholeheartedly agreed with my side of the case. Because I had pled guilty, he had no choice but to punish me somehow, but he gave me the lightest possible sentence: a fine of $750,000 and only five days in US custody, even stipulating that I didn't have to do all five days at once. After that, I'd be on probation for a year.

"The reason I picked five days is because the message the five days sends, to almost everybody who sees this, that it's a regrettable moment but not a signal of significant criminality for wrongdoing," said the judge. "As five days is the kind of sentence you give somebody who has stepped a little over the line, that's the way it will be received and read. . . . I think he started out with a mistake which turned out not to be a mistake, but a crime. And I think he didn't do it because it didn't seem particularly large or significant, and in the real world it's probably not large or significant. He got to the position that some people do and that is, you open the wrong door and there's no way to go back through the door, take whatever sin you committed with you and return it some place that does no harm. Once it's done, it can't be taken back."

I didn't fully comprehend what the judge was saying, except for the next bit, which probably meant almost as much to me as my short sentence. "I'm sorry about what happened with the rifles," the judge said. "I know that I would not be on any Olympic team, but it takes enormous concentration and complete attention to do it."

I felt not only great relief when the gavel fell to adjourn the court, but understood by that judge and therefore a little less alone. He was right in saying this court case had been like an albatross around my neck. As I'd told him in my parole letter, my goal was to present myself before him with "the most honesty as possible," asking for his mercy.

The judge had granted me that mercy, and in doing so taught me that, sometimes, in your darkest hour, other people will come

231

Four Days in Court

through for you, particularly if you're open about the mistakes you've made. By laying my whole life story before him, the judge believed, as I'd told him, that my mistake in judgment was "just one blemish in a life that has been filled with hard work and honesty and doing things the right way."

The lesson here is that, if you are honest with people—as I had been with Webster and the Amish, and later with Darlington Dairy Supply and the bank, and now the judge—people will believe in you.

Chapter 14

Prison Days and Finding Grace

Belong to a Group, but Keep Your Own Counsel.

I f nothing else, my chaotic Mexican childhood had handed me one golden ticket: a lack of medical forms. When I was given a routine tuberculosis test during the required government physical prior to serving my jail sentence and it turned out to be positive, the doctor asked to see my vaccination forms from childhood.

"I don't have them," I said.

"Well, can you get them?"

"I doubt it," I said. "My father's dead and my mother has moved many times."

In the end, the prison warden had no choice but to put me in a jail cell by myself, "for health and safety" reasons. At least I wouldn't have to worry about being knifed in my sleep, I thought.

My first day in prison, I walked in slowly, feeling strong and fit because of the Krav Maga training, but wary just the same. Prison in real life looks just like prison in the movies. There are long rows of cells, and when they close the door behind you, you're trapped in a tiny room with a bed, a sink, a toilet, and a roll of toilet paper, all behind a small door with bars over the window. I heaved a sigh of relief when I saw that I would be alone and sank onto the bed.

There are many downsides to being locked up like an animal in a cage, of course; one of the biggest is that it takes forever for one minute to go by when you're deprived of your liberty. The upside was that the routines were easy to follow, with prescribed times in the exercise yard and in the lunchroom. The only hitch for me was when I was leaving the cafeteria line with my tray that first day and deciding where to sit. A White guy with the usual array of terrible tattoos asked me which group I belonged to.

"What do you mean?" I asked, bristling. At first I thought he was asking about gangs.

"You know. Black, Mexican, Italian. What are you?"

"Oh. I'm from Mexico."

He nodded and gestured toward a table of men with his chin. "Then you should sit with the Mexicans."

"Why?"

"Because one person alone is not good in prison. You have to belong to a group."

"Okay. Thanks," I said, and walked over to that table.

The trick to staying safe in prison, I discovered, was to belong to a group, yes, but to keep to your own counsel as well. My Krav Maga teacher had given me this advice: "Don't make conversation with anyone, Miguel. Meet their eyes, but don't look at them for too long. You don't want to intimidate anyone, and staring into someone's eyes can make that person feel threatened."

In the University of Life, jail is one of the toughest master's degrees. They own your freedom. Whoever you are when you're locked up, it will change you one way or another.

In my case, being in jail taught me to examine every problem from multiple angles to avoid making a mistake that could result in me pissing off the guards or inmates and ending up having to stay longer. Overall, prison taught me patience—never had the hours been so long—but other important lessons as well. I learned how to read people by paying attention to every action and glance. I also learned to be alert and not to depend on anyone.

My childhood had taught me I could only truly depend on myself, and now, after Martina's betrayal, I vowed to remember that lesson well. For the first time I found I could control all of my fears because I was fully alert and dedicated to remaining calm. I had at last subdued The Transformer within me.

The only person who came to visit me during that time was my friend Jorge; he came to pick me up when I was released, too. We celebrated by eating lunch at Tacos La Iguana, where I ordered six tacos and thought I'd never felt happier.

The ordeal was over. At last I could turn the page and start my new life. All I had to decide was what to do with it.

■ ■ ■

It's difficult to feel positive about your life when you don't know how to live in the present. My mind kept pulling me back into the past, to a time when I was a workaholic. You know those Energizer Bunny TV commercials? That was me, in constant motion. Now that I was out of prison, now that all of that was behind me, I had to figure out how to live to a different rhythm of life, one that was slower and more meaningful, so I could pay more attention to myself and to the people I loved. I had to focus on the present moment.

One of the first positive steps I took after prison was to contact my children and invite them to celebrate Christmas with me at my apartment with Jorge and his children.

"Please," I said. "It would mean so much to me if we spent the holiday together."

To my immense relief, they agreed. It helped that my children and Jorge's kids were all friends. We spent two days together, eating and drinking and opening gifts. Cristobal kept his distance from me, and things were quiet and strained between us, but I tried to simply enjoy the holiday and my children. Somehow we managed to keep the peace.

Prison Days and Finding Grace

One day, we would have to talk about their mother and me, and what really happened, but this wasn't the time.

■ ■ ■

When I was finally able to travel, naturally the first place I went was Mexico to see my family. I had been worried about my mother. Reports from my family and friends in Irapuato described how she was suffering from dementia and they'd put her in a nursing home. I hadn't been able to spend any time with her for years. First, because I was too busy with work, and because Martina seemed to arrange our trips so that we spent most of our holidays in Mexico with her family, and then because I had to wait for the trial and my prison sentence to be over.

It felt strange, being able to travel freely, but it was wonderful. I was eager to enjoy myself in Mexico and reconnect with everyone. However, when I arrived in Irapuato, where I was expecting a grand family reunion, I discovered that everything had gone to hell. While I had been waiting for the trial, my mother had fallen and hit her head; this seemed to have caused her dementia symptoms to accelerate. She had no idea who I was and could barely speak.

I had been feeling close to my family, and grateful to them for supporting me during the trial, but now that I was in Mexico, I realized that the $3,000 stipends I'd been paying each of them to support their health insurance had all gone to other things. Not one of my siblings had actually bought health insurance with the money. This made me angry, as did the fact that none of them seemed to be taking responsibility for my mother's care. Instead, they'd put her in a nursing home that I was paying for—and they didn't even visit, according to the aides.

I immediately moved my mother back into her own apartment and hired 24/7 aides to be with her, under my sister's supervision. Still, I was determined to be closer to my brothers, to share some of

The House that Cheese Built

my experiences with them and find out what had really been going on in their lives during the years I'd been stranded in the United States awaiting the trial, so I suggested a family vacation.

"How about if I treat you all to a trip?" I suggested. "Just us siblings. Let's have a family reunion in Puerto Vallarta."

"And you'll pay for everything?" Pedro asked anxiously.

"Yes, of course."

They agreed to accompany me on an all-expenses paid vacation to Puerto Vallarta, not knowing, of course, that I was orchestrating a sort of intensive family therapy session. I thought we had the best chance of talking honestly to one another in a setting of enforced togetherness, so I hit on the idea of renting a boat with a chef for one day of our vacation. If somebody got tired of talking about heavy issues, well, they would have to jump overboard.

They almost did. My brothers had absolutely no inclination to talk about anything unpleasant. Certainly they weren't about to reveal any of their feelings about our father and our often violent childhood or about our mother's dementia or even about Martina and what she'd done to try and destroy me and our family. All my brothers wanted to do on our vacation was what they always wanted to do: drink and get high and have a good time.

By the end of the vacation, I had concluded, once again, that I was the family outcast. There was no place for me among the Leal brothers. Nobody loved us the way parents should love and guide their children, so each of us had to raise ourselves. Either I'd been different from the start, or my experiences of living in the United States and creating a successful company had transformed me into someone my brothers saw not as a blood relative, but as a piggy bank.

■ ■ ■

My brother Pedro and I went into business together after that. I gave him the money to build some houses and sell them, and I kept

14 acres of land so I could build my own house and start a small farm. It's clear to me now—abundantly so—that I had been seeing my life through Martina's eyes, not through my own. I had been living life to make her happy and to provide for my children. Now it was time for me to imagine a different kind of life, one where the visions and goals are purely my own.

After moving to my farm in Mexico, I started a simple daily routine to cleanse my mind and keep me strong: running or going to the gym, then visiting my mom and having breakfast with her. Afterward, I would visit the building site for my new house, where I would meet with contractors and painters.

After interviewing several locals, I chose a business partner for my farm, a young man named Ricardo, who was interested in learning more about organic farming. Organic farming techniques are still in the infancy stage in Mexico, and I decided that would be my next venture: using the land I'd bought around my house to teach Ricardo and others in my village how to grow vegetables in the healthiest, most sustainable way possible.

If that goes well—and I think it will, since we just won the area's top agricultural prize for our strawberries—then my next step will be to build a barn and start a farm-to-table restaurant, which will employ local people, draw tourists, and teach the community about organic farming practices. I also have plans to grow more avocados; I'm currently planting trees to see how they do in our soil, and I'm exploring the idea of mezcal production. I'm also developing an exciting new recipe for queso fresco that promises to be even better than the one I created at the height of my career.

In addition, I am intent on laying a path forward for the women in my community who have helped my mother by paying for scholarships to reward them for taking such good care of her. One is studying to become a chef, another is going to school to style hair, and a third will earn her college degree. My goal is to help them study and have careers so they can support themselves and have better opportunities. I have also paid for the health care and scholarships for children in town who suffer from a genetic disease. Who wants to be the richest man buried in the cemetery? Not me.

Happiness is a complicated business. What has kept me from being happy, I've slowly realized, wasn't what happened with Martina or the lawsuit. It was *me*. It doesn't matter where I am or what I'm doing. I've learned that happiness must be something I cultivate within myself.

The most important thing I can do is take care in whom I trust with my heart and guard my true self from being too malleable. I hope that anyone I meet now will see that I am true to my own visions and values. I listen to other people more than I talk, and live with gratitude for the smallest everyday moments. I will keep going forward with my creative ideas, because for me, creativity is a path to happiness.

Money has not changed the fact that I am a simple man. I dress the same way I always did and I don't need a new car every 10 minutes. I'm glad I have enough money to live comfortably, but I know I can't take it with me. I hope to leave a legacy, the sort of project like my organic farm, that can nurture many people and make my hometown of Irapuato, and Mexico, a better place for all.

Epilogue: Key Lessons for Entrepreneurs

The Recipe for Paying Attention to Opportunity.

There are certain things nobody can teach you about life. For instance, only you can decide whom you want to marry or choose as a life partner, and only you can decide if you want children. You're also the only one who can decide what career you want to pursue because you know best where your talents and passions lie.

However, whether you're an immigrant or grew up in the United States, whether you're building a business for the first time or already an experienced entrepreneur, certain key lessons will help you realize your dream.

Starting a business is a little like running a marathon: you need to expect to train hard and be in top form, both physically and mentally, so you can dig in for the long haul. Be prepared to sweat and stumble on your way to the finish line. Creating a company is hard work. Entrepreneurs must be as resilient and realistic as they are starry-eyed and optimistic.

I don't say this to discourage you. My aim is to help you start your own business with your eyes wide open, so you can enjoy the same success I have. If you build a business in the United States, you will likely become wealthier than you could any other way, but even if you fail, the lessons you learn will be invaluable. You will carry that knowledge forward into your life.

Here are some of the most valuable lessons I've learned on my way from being an hourly factory worker to a cheesemaker with a multi-million-dollar business of my own.

1. Hard Times Can Be Your Best Teachers.

All entrepreneurs have unique journeys. So did I, and so will you. It took me years of working low-paid, hourly factory jobs to realize that becoming a cheesemaker might be a viable career. I faced hard times along the way, like having no money or English skills when I first landed in the United States, and learning the ins and outs of what it means to grow a company from the ground up.

Would things have gone more easily if I'd had more resources, like a college degree and parents who supported me? Sure. On the other hand, because I had no means of support other than my own wits, I became adept at watching other people and learning through observation and experience.

Being hungry and poor also meant that I didn't spend my money on luxuries like eating out or drinking after work like a lot of my coworkers. Desperate to better myself, I applied a laser-like focus to every task in front of me, learning what I needed to know. All of that was great preparation for the long days and nights I'd have to put in when it was time to launch my own business.

2. Be Your Own Best Customer and Make Something People Want.

If you want to succeed in producing something the marketplace wants, be your own best customer. Think about what you want that isn't already out there. In my case, I was homesick for the language, smells, food, and people from Mexico, and I realized that a lot of the Mexican immigrants coming into the United States probably felt the same way. By producing the cotija cheese they were accustomed to, and longing for, I created a product that was an instant hit.

From there, I applied the same strategy to growing my business that I'd always applied to other areas in my life, like competitive shooting: I focused hardest on competing against myself and earning better scores. When it came to producing cheese, I didn't worry about what my competitors were making. Instead, I listened carefully to what my customers wanted to add to their own stores, refrigerators, or pantry shelves. Focusing on the marketplace and testing what your customers want is a much surer strategy for growth than trying to outsmart your competitors.

3. Take Satisfaction in Achieving Small Steps Toward Your Goal.

Most entrepreneurs have some kind of end goal. For instance, I might have dreamed of one day selling my business for millions of dollars, but I didn't know enough to do that. In my experience, that was for the best. Thinking too far ahead can cause you to stumble and give up because it makes your goals seem impossible to reach.

Instead, set small, incremental goals that are realistic to achieve. You'll make steady progress that way. I compare this to making a perfect cheese. I might try a recipe that's almost the right one, and that's a cause for celebration. But before taking that cheese to market, I would tweak the recipe many times to make sure I had exactly the right flavor and texture. Along the way, I'd take joy in small accomplishments, like finding exactly the right piece of equipment to make production easier or establishing a new sales route for distribution. All of these small steps were crucial steppingstones to my eventual success.

4. Get Your Emotions Under Control Before Making Important Decisions.

In the business arena, just like in every other part of your life, certain events will spark strong emotions. You know what that feels like. Maybe an employee embezzles money, or a trusted partner stabs you in the back, and you find yourself obsessing over what happened. Your vision tunnels, and you can scarcely breathe because tension is like a lasso around your ribs. It's easy to hate those people who did you wrong or betrayed you in some way. You might even want to seek revenge by posting about it on social media, firing everyone associated with that person, or worse.

But no good business decisions can be made in that kind of emotional state. Pause and take a breath. When you're calm, consider your options, actions, and potential consequences. Then act.

5. Everything in Life Happens for a Reason—Even Obstacles.

Whenever you launch a new business—or even a new product line—you will hit roadblocks. Some of these might be personal, like maybe you don't feel enough passion for your endeavor to keep going. Other obstacles will be practical ones, like you can't get the funding you need for a prototype, or you can't reach your target goal of a hundred customers to prove to investors that you have a solid idea. In my own path to creating a multi-million-dollar company, my roadblocks started with not knowing the language, not being a citizen, and having no idea how businesses operated in the United States. Any one of these obstacles could have caused me to stop and say, "I can't do it."

Instead of letting myself quit, I persisted, tackling one roadblock at a time and viewing each obstacle as a new learning opportunity. If there wasn't one way to do something, I found another. For example, the first time Webster and I made cheese ourselves and took it to customers outside of Chicago, we realized we couldn't keep up with the pace. I took a step back, reassessed, and seized the next opportunity that came along, which was exporting and selling used dairy equipment from the United States to Mexico. Doing that gave me the money I needed to become a partner in the first cheese-making factory I had ever worked in as a teenager, which led to my next, bigger opportunity to make cheese with a company in the United States.

Practice saying yes to new opportunities whenever you confront a roadblock. Sometimes, if it's hard to jump over an obstacle, people make the mistake of not moving because they're afraid of falling down. But if you want to succeed in business, you must keep finding new ways to push through obstacles, hurdle over them, or go around them one step at a time until you reach your desired destination.

6. Let Failure Inspire You.

My father was a smart, creative man who often dreamed of doing things, but his dreams always died at the stage where he sketched them on napkins because actually putting them into action seemed too difficult.

The thing is, your business ideas are worthless if you never see them through. If you don't risk anything, you'll fail for sure because you'll never get your business off the ground. The only way to learn is by doing. Don't make excuses, hoping someone else will come along and do the hard work for you. Take joy in learning from your mistakes and let failure inspire you. Otherwise, life will likely keep hitting you in the same spot. Each problem you resolve is a learning experience.

7. **The Rhythms of Life Will Change as You Succeed, but Stay Alert.**

Imagine your business as a tiny snowball and you're pushing it up a mountain. The higher you get on the mountain, the more snow you gather (and maybe some rocks, too). As the snowball gets bigger and bigger, it will take more effort to keep pushing it up the mountain. Finally you reach the summit, and suddenly your journey is a downhill one.

However, even though your effort will change—you will no longer be pushing that snowball to maintain momentum—you can't take your eye off the snowball. You'll have to direct it around boulders and curves in the path, or it'll go flying off a cliff or smash into something. The rhythm of your life as a business owner will change, but it will still require you to stay on alert for the next obstacles.

8. **Happiness and Success Are Never Permanent, and Are Not Tied to Ambition or Wealth.**

Happiness and success are intangible things. Only you can define what they mean to you, and those definitions will likely shift over time. When I first started out in life, I defined happiness as marrying my first love and having a family with her. Success, to me, meant being able to provide for my family in ways my own father had failed to do for ours when I was a child. I never imagined I'd be living the American Dream, owning a business and having enough money to buy whatever I wanted.

Gradually, I realized that my definition of happiness had been based on something false. After my wife's betrayal and our divorce, I was forced to reassess my own values and start my life over. A fulfilling career is never about the money, in the end, but about realizing your true passions. The same is true of relationships.

If you constantly try to make another person happy and live your life for that person, you will lose yourself. Your own happiness and success can never be tied to another person's vision for your life or to ambition or wealth. They must be based on creative satisfaction and good relationships and can only spring from within yourself.

9. To Succeed in Business, You Need to Persuade Others to Take a Risk on You.

How do you appear trustworthy to business partners? Develop a strong, consistent personal brand that evokes confidence in everyone around you, especially financial partners. This means demonstrating consistent reliability in your ethics and consistency in how you show up.

Never take shortcuts in delivering the best possible product. Others are more likely to take a risk on you if they feel confident that the end product will be top quality and delivered on time.

10. Develop an Exit Strategy.

Eventually, you will need to exit the company you've created and grown. Your exit strategy should be based on examining your own physical and mental health, whether you're in a position to build a legacy company for future generations, and evaluating whether you have money enough to live according to your own needs and values—not some arbitrary dollar amount.

The Surefire Recipe for Paying Attention to Opportunity

I've illustrated many of these ingredients with illustrations from my own life story in this book, but here is my recipe for paying attention to opportunity:

Desire Better: You have to *want* to improve your situation.

Respect Your Body: Stay away from mind-altering or mind-numbing activities like alcohol and drugs, which can distract and dull your mindset.

Avoid Frivolous Friends: People who aren't focused on improving their own situations will be a distraction.

Save Money: Always save money because worrying about not having enough of it can impact your ability to pay attention.

Be Ruthless with Your Time and Energy: Eliminate all distractions that impact your ability to focus on getting ahead.

Create Opportunity: Don't wait for opportunities to find you. Create them for yourself.

Be Stubborn: Maintain a mindset of "making it happen" no matter what obstacles fall in your way.

Push for 1% More: Try to achieve more every day, even if it's only 1% more.

Seek Out New Data: Always find ways to better yourself through new skills and education.

One Goal at a Time: Focusing on one goal at a time is the best way to channel your energy before moving on to a new goal.

Epilogue: Key Lessons for Entrepreneurs

About the Author

Miguel Leal is widely regarded as the "godfather of Mexican cheese" in the United States. He is an entrepreneur with a history of business management experience.

Mr. Leal immigrated to the Unites States from Mexico as a teenager for an apprenticeship at a cheese factory in Wisconsin, launching his career in cheese making that culminated in building his own cheese factory, from which he introduced various Mexican cheeses (most from his own recipes) across the country. He not only cultivated recipes for Mexican cheeses, he invented and patented machinery for cheese production.

Increased immigration from Mexico to the United States during the early 1990s sparked his interest in these endeavors. Mr. Leal saw this trend as the prelude to a new market for Mexican cheese and subsequently partnered with a master cheesemaker to produce and sell wheels of cotija cheese. In response to rising demand, Mr. Leal opened Mexican Cheese Producers in 1994.

Today, Miguel Leal serves as a real estate developer. His properties include La Giralda Residencial, a subdivision in Irapuato, Mexico, consisting of 150 single-family homes. Additionally, he divides his time between real estate ventures and his passion project of supporting the organic food movement in Mexico. To this end, he oversees a farm of his own to aid local charitable efforts and provide communities in Mexico with demonstrations of sustainable practices for organic farming.

Mr. Leal's factory continues to use his recipes and earn commendations for its cheese. In 2020, its cotija cheese earned "best in class" accolades at the World Championship Cheese Contest.

About the Author

Index

256

Index